Cape Breton's
Christmas

BOOK TEN

A Treasury
of Stories and Memories

Edited by

Ronald Caplan

Breton Books

Front Cover Painting by Gary LeDrew, www.garyledrew.com
Back Cover Painting "Kalckreuth Children by the Christmas tree" by
Leopold Graf von Kalckreuth (1855–1928).

Our thanks to Hélène D'Amour for permission to use Ludger D'Amour's
story, "The Blessing of the Beggar." It appeared in *The Runaway*, a short
story collection edited by Antonio D'Amour. "Christmas . . . New and
Improved" and "Take My Turkey . . . Please!" were published in *The Nova
Scotian*, a weekend supplement to the *Chronicle Herald*, and in Donna Doyle
D'Amour's book *Colouring the Road—Adventures in Everyday Life*.

Thanks to Tom Ross for "Faceplant" from *In the Bleak Midwinter:
Christmas Tales of Hope from the Homeless, Addicted, and Afflicted*.

Archie Neil Chisholm's "There was always food and fiddling" is from
Partici-Paper, November/December 1995.

"Lessons of Life and Leadership from the Real Saint Nicholas" from *In
the Public Square: A Citizen's Reader* by Tom Urbaniak, Breton Books, 2023.

Our thanks to McGraw Hill Canada for permission to publish
"Stilly Night" from *The Best of Gregory Clark*, copyright McGraw-Hill
Ryerson Ltd., January 1959, ISBN-10 : 0770060242 and ISBN-13 :
978-0770060244.

Our thanks to Warren Gordon for sharing Cape Breton background for
the story "Stilly Night." And thanks as well to Captain Darrel C. Leighton,
president of the West Nova Regiment Association, Sgt. rtd., Garry Landry
and Capt. Joshua O'Keefe, adjutant, West Nova Scotia Regiment, for their
help in locating the text for "Stilly Night," and keeping the story alive.

We recognize the support of the Province of Nova Scotia.
We are pleased to work in partnership with the Province of
Nova Scotia to develop and promote our creative industries for
the benefit of all Nova Scotians.

Funded by the Government of Canada. | Canadä

Library and Archives Canada Cataloguing in Publication.

Title: Cape Breton's Christmas : a treasury of stories and memories / edited
with an introduction by Ronald Caplan.
Names: Caplan, Ronald, 1942- editor.
Identifiers: Canadiana 20149065310 | ISBN 9781998919048 (vol. 10;
softcover)
Subjects: LCSH: Christmas—Nova Scotia—Cape Breton Island—Literary
collections. | LCSH: Cape Breton Island (N.S.)—Literary collections.
| CSH: Canadian literature (English) Nova Scotia—Cape Breton Island.
| CSH: Canadian literature (English)—21st century. | LCGFT:
Christmas fiction.
Classification: LCC PS8237.C57 C38 2014 | DDC C810.8/0334—dc23

Printed in Canada

Contents

Last Christmas

Octavia Panthier

It **was December 25th**—Christmas morning. As usual, Octavia woke up extra early. In the years before, she'd awakened crazy excited, energized, jumping around, and waking up everyone in the house. This Christmas wasn't like that.

She woke up and felt nothing. The decorations were up—the fairy lights, the candles, the little forest animals, and the crafts that she and her sister had made in daycare from pipe cleaners, glitter, and glue. Her mom hadn't put up the tree that year because there were too many pets and people gathering. The whole family had come to celebrate, but it was also something more.

Octavia didn't feel that automatic spark of energy and joy that she usually did as a kid on Christmas morning. When she was little, it felt like everyone she loved would live forever. This year, she'd started to worry that would not be the case. Her mom had been caring for a dear and close friend who was very ill, and all of the adults seemed weary and burdened by life's troubles—a global pandemic, tight money worries, foreign wars, raging storms, and bad diagnoses. She wanted to make things calm, simple, and easy for everyone, even though she was still just a kid and couldn't fix the world's problems any more than she could turn back time. She put on a smile and treated it like a regular Christmas morning.

Slowly, the family gathered in the living room. The big black dog from Boston who had just been rescued from city streets down south seemed delighted to receive a squeaky avocado from a vegan relative and a honking goose from a fellow carnivore. His big tail thumped the floor, and he slobbered over his new toys, scaring the cat who was hiding in the basement.

Octavia made a pile of her gifts too. She wondered if her mom's friend, who had grown so frail, would ever be able to use the lavender bath salts she received.

After sharing the presents and some breakfast treats, cinnamon rolls and fruit salad, Christmas still didn't feel the same as before. She had thought maybe her feelings would change after the giving and receiving of gifts, but she still felt more solemn than celebratory.

The family spread out around the house, checking messages, making phone calls, and cleaning up. They began cooking Christmas dinner and chatting about the usual topics—how to prepare the food, who was having trouble at work, would the weather mess with travel plans.

Octavia and her older sister took their little cousin to watch "The Christmas Chronicles" in the bedroom. The cousin from Boston jumped on the bed and made everyone laugh. All Octavia could think about were the possible reasons why she wasn't able to joke around and get as excited this Christmas.

She went out into the kitchen. Her big, tall grandpa was deep in conversation with her mom's tiny, pale friend. She was surprised to see them so animated as they debated world events. Despite everything, they were laughing.

Grandpa put his arm around Octavia and kissed her on the forehead. His familiar presence relaxed her heart.

She was growing older, entering her early teenage years, and Christmas just didn't have the same spark as it had when she was younger. There were many reasons for this. She felt disappointed and a little bit guilty for losing her child self, the little girl who used to jump on the bed with her cousin. Everyone had done their best to make Christmas as special as possible during a hard time. She leaned on her grandfather's shoulder and was glad he still made her feel safe.

Even after the family had gone home—and her mom's friend had died—she continued to think about that special sad Christmas. She couldn't go back and change the feelings she had that Christmas day, but she could learn from them. Sometimes memories are rosier than reality. Maybe that Christmas was, in its own way, just as joyful or even more joyful than the previous ones. She had spent the day with the people that filled her heart with infinite joy and love. Heartache would be a part of that as she grew older and wiser, but she knew that she would find it in herself to celebrate again, like the rescue pup with his squeaky avocado and her boisterous cousin jumping up and down on the messy bed.

A Christmas Wish

Sharon Dunn

I was in Grade 12 at Holy Angels High School in Sydney, and we were preparing the deliveries for the annual Christmas drive. Every year, each classroom was given a needy family to help for Christmas. Some classes gathered more items than others, but every family was guaranteed a Christmas dinner paid for by the student council, even if a class hadn't raised enough funds.

It was Christmas Eve and I was going to be driving one of the delivery trucks. I had two students to help me. We were given two deliveries. One was very small consisting of only two boxes—one box with a donated turkey and the other containing some trimmings for dinner.

I checked the notes, it said a family of four—mom, dad

and two children, a boy aged four and a girl of five. The other delivery was massive. It was for a mom, dad and several teenage boys. Their assigned class had really put it together. Not only Christmas dinner, but clothes, sports equipment, blankets, games and canned food to last months. There must have been fifty boxes. We packed the truck and I kept the two boxes for the first family in the front seat with me.

"We'll deliver the small order first," I advised the girls. The address was close by. "And then we can focus on the second, large delivery."

We quickly arrived at the tenement address, and I knocked loudly on the door. It was answered by a slim woman who looked old to me, a seventeen-year-old, but I would guess now that she was probably in her late twenties. She seemed tired and nervous. I remember her hair high in a bun, and her nylon stockings rolled down to her ankles, the way some women wore them back then.

We went up the stairway to arrive at her sparsely decorated flat with our two meagre boxes. I could see that she didn't have much, but her place was spotless. "I love your tree," I told her. "It doesn't have many decorations," she apologised. "No, it's beautiful," I insisted, and it was.

Sitting in front of the tree were her two adorable young children dressed in their Sunday best. They looked shy and scared. I didn't know what was going on here, but I knew that something was definitely off. I scanned the room and saw a man in an armchair in a corner, obviously the dad. He didn't look well and he didn't say a word. I assumed that he was sick, but now I think that he was an alcoholic, which is of course a disease in itself, and which would explain the atmosphere in the room.

The woman was very grateful for what we had brought, and thanked us profusely.

"I'm so sorry we don't have more," I told her.

"No, this is perfect," she insisted. But I could see that things were far from perfect. She and I had connected when she had first opened the door and as she looked at me now, I felt that she was trying to tell me something. But what?

We said our goodbyes and left, and as we got back in the car, we were all downcast about what we had seen. We were silent as we headed for our next destination, in a rural area. When we arrived there, we had to trek through a long driveway that hadn't been shovelled, with snow up to our knees, and when we finally made it to the kitchen we started to pile the boxes in a cramped room. I asked a couple of the older teens if they could help us bring the rest of the boxes in from the car. They refused. As we headed outside, still quiet and sad about the first delivery, I asked, "Is anyone thinking what I'm thinking?" Both girls said, "Yup." "Okay," I told them, "we're going to deliver most of the boxes here but we're going to save a few and go back to the other house, right?" They both nodded.

We were happy and laughing on the drive back to the first house. I rapped on the door and when the surprised woman appeared, we said that we had forgotten to bring up a few things. We happily marched past her with a slew of boxes containing lots of canned goods, blankets, and even Christmas ornaments. We were so proud of ourselves, we thought we were heroes. But the woman seemed even more perplexed than before, as she looked for places to put all of the loot. I could see that, try as we may, we weren't solving her problem.

I took her aside, and said quietly. "How can I help you?" With tears in her eyes, she told me that she had no toys for her children, and then it dawned on me that in all of the boxes we delivered, there wasn't one toy! They had missed it at the school and we had missed it as well. "What do they want?" I asked her. "My daughter wants a doll and my son wants a firetruck," she said helplessly, "but you've done too much," she added, tears now streaming down her face. "I'll be back," I promised.

As we left, I was worried because day was quickly turning into night, and the stores were closing soon. But I remembered that every Christmas Eve, my dad would make a final run to the shops.

I got home as fast as I could. "I'm going out with you, Dad," I told him. "No, Sharon, I'm going alone," he said. I explained the situation. "I can't take on anything else, I've got five kids," Dad moaned.

"Dad, remember when you told me that your uncle would drink and throw the Christmas tree out on Christmas Eve?" He nodded. "Well, that's the kind of Christmas these kids are about to have." That's all I needed to say. "Let's go," Dad said.

We jumped in the car and headed to the stores, and after getting what he needed for our family, we were able to find a small fire truck, a cute doll, a skipping rope, and a *Snakes and Ladders* game for the little family. Dad added some colouring books and crayons, Christmas candy and chocolates.

We headed back to their house in the blinding snow, and stopped at the front. I left their pile on the step and then I banged on the door. Dad yelled, "Merry Christmas, ho, ho ho," in his best Santa Claus voice, and we peeled away. We went around the block and when we returned the gifts had been retrieved and I saw a light on in the hallway.

I imagined the scene inside, and hoped that Mom and the kids, and Dad too, felt less pressured now. And after all of our shenanigans and our efforts that day, the wonderful Mom finally had the only thing she had ever wanted—her children's wishes come true.

My Christmas Memories

Laverne MacRae

It was Christmas Eve 1963. We were sitting in to supper around five p.m. Supper was always at five.

We kids—or some of us—were listening sharply to the radio for Santa's whereabouts. We were a house full of kids—six at that time—and I was the second oldest. My two younger brothers teased me as I shushed them to listen to the radio as to when Santa was coming to us. They both said, "Santa's not coming to you."

Well I was a pretty serious kid, and a good kid, I thought— my oldest sister and I getting all our chores done every day as mother's helpers. Coming first in my class of three in our one-room school. Of course, I was a good kid, and Santa would be coming to me, and I told them so.

"He is coming to me and bringing me a baking set!" I told them right off.

I loved dolls but there was no more room in our bed that I shared with Val. I had seen a baking set in the Christmas cata- logue. Didn't we love going through the Christmas Eatons and Sears catalogues in those days! Then our mother said, "Well, you never told us that!" I am thinking, "Well, why would I tell *you* that?"—but that would have been talking back, so I said nothing.

On Christmas Eve we were sent to bed around six, as Santa would not come if he saw us up. I suppose we were told that to get us from underfoot.

The kitchen floor would then be scrubbed and waxed for sure, and the tree decorated. Oh, the work that a woman would do!

Then at noon she would produce the perfect Christmas

dinner with all the trimmings, after getting up in the early morning hours to get the turkey stuffed and in the oven. My parents always gave us a great Christmas.

Some of us would have gone to the woods with Dad earlier in the day, following in his big foot holes to get our tree. He loved Christmas and oh, the wonderful smell of that tree when he brought it in.

One year Dad borrowed a hundred dollars to make Christmas for us, and that included the turkey. Weeks later I overheard him telling Mom he was having a hard time paying it back and wished he hadn't done it. I felt sad for him.

After we were in bed, Mom decorated the tree. Imagine! Some ornaments were glass so she must have been scared that we might break them. And that would have been her quiet time. For his part, Dad would have already put the Christmas tree lights on.

This particular year we had lights on our tree! Electricity was in our house for the first time ever. We lived up a dirt road and a long lane so it was very costly to get power up the Barlow Road. To have electricity—that was really exciting in 1963. A few years later came a bathroom and double stainless steel sinks and taps in the kitchen. Out with the hand pump and other unmentionables, but the kitchen wood stove stood its ground for our mother, who needed it and loved to bake.

"Do you think we'll ever see dirty dishes again, Lorne?" she would say to Dad, because now we all loved doing the dishes and turning on the taps and having water coming out hot or cold depending which knob we turned. Even the little ones standing or kneeling on a kitchen chair—this was a great way to keep them entertained.

Well, after we kids were in bed on this magical evening all around the world, my father must have slipped out of the house. Christmas morning came and there was my baking set beside my stocking! My baking set! Santa brought me a baking set just like I wanted from the catalogue. A little wooden rolling pin with red handles, tiny animal cookie cutters, an egg beater and little red mixing bowls. I was overjoyed with my gift from Santa.

It was a few years later that I put it all together that Dad had gone up the road to the Arsenault & Gaudet general store and asked the owner to open up because he needed a baking set for one of his kids. It would not be open at that hour on Christmas Eve.

Today I'm a grown woman but at Christmastime still there is a version of that little ten-year-old girl inside. I have a small brown pottery bowl and put out my collected pieces of a children's baking set, to remind me of that wonderful Christmas morning that I got my baking set! The original baking set is long gone, so when I am out and about at my favorite antique shops, yard sales or the reuse centre, if I see bits of a child's baking set, I smile. I usually leave it behind for someone else as I have enough in my baking bowl.

Seeing my baking set memory collection gives me joy all through the Christmas holiday season. My bowl is pleasantly full and my heart is full at Christmas time of mostly good memories. Well, I was a good girl and that proved it !

There is no Santa Claus. Humbug! There is!

A few years ago I was asked by our local Lions Club in Baddeck to play the role of Mrs. Santa Claus beside Mr. Santa Claus. I had long silver hair then. We saw over a hundred children that day and had such fun. This dear child in a red velvet dress asked me if she was a good child. Oh dear! I think I hugged her as she tugged at my heart strings. "Yes, you are a very good child." She smiled shyly at me and moved on, pleased with herself.

Of all the children we saw that day, I remember her the most. Oh my, why do we teasingly bribe children, I thought. Gosh, did I do that to my children too? I will have to ask.

I will leave you with this famous family quip of our father, the man that worked so hard to provide. My parents ended up with eight children and of course when the twenty-pound turkey arrived at the table we all wanted a leg. My father would say, "It's a turkey not a spider!"

Christmas at the Cove

Colleen Gillis

I'm blessed to belong to a folk choir who sing for the Saturday evening Mass at Holy Redeemer Church in Whitney Pier. A few weeks before Christmas 2022, our director, Delores, asked if we would like to sing Christmas carols for the residents at the Cove Guest Home. We happily agreed.

On a crisp and cold Sunday afternoon, eight of us showed up at the Cove. While Kevin, Leona and Jule tuned their guitars, the MacAskill Room began to fill up with folks with walkers and wheelchairs and a few under their own steam. About twenty-five in all. From the moment we launched into "Sleigh bells ring, are you listening . . . ," we were on key and in good harmony. Judging from the response of some of the residents, they agreed.

Granted, some of them were either dozing or wearing deadpan faces. Halfway through our performance, one glum-looking elderly woman turned her wheelchair around and slowly but surely headed for the exit, with a staff person in hot pursuit. However, the rest of the residents stayed for the whole hour, with some singing along and clapping. One woman requested "O Come All Ye Faithful" and another wanted "Silent Night," both of which we gladly sang. One very loud, enthusiastic woman kept saying, "I like you! Come again!"

As we said our good-byes, with lots of thanks, a few hugs and tears, I was thrilled that we took the time and energy to bring a little Christmas spirit to the folks at the Cove. They actually did us a favour by showing so much appreciation. And in response to that loud, enthusiastic woman, I said, "I like you too! We will come again!"

I sincerely hope we do.

Eat and Eat Again

Taiya Barss

I have index cards on the side of my fridge, with a few favourite and often-used recipes. "Best Pizza," "How to Cook Oatmeal," and "Deb's Cukes."

"Peel and slice two English cucumbers, place in a bowl, sprinkling salt in between the layers. Cover with a small plate, a stone on top of the plate to weigh it down, and leave for two or three hours. Drain, pour over it 1/2 cup vinegar mixed with 1/4 cup sugar, let chill, drain again, add a grind of pepper, and serve."

They stay crisp for days.

It is the only way I ever eat cucumbers.

They are a small part of a huge meal, a Swedish smorgasbord that my friend Deb prepares every Christmas. My grandchildren call me Granny; her children called her mother Mormor, the Swedish word that means the same.

The food, the gathering of friends to share the food, keeps the Swedish blood flowing through the family's veins.

Preparations for the feast start long before the holidays. Sausage to be made, barley to simmer in the savoury meat juices until tender, rye bread, pickled beets and cucumbers, relishes, seasoned kidney beans. Meatballs—Swedish meatballs, of course—head cheese, tart lingonberry sauce, pickled herring, deviled eggs, sliced ham and cheeses.

Pick any three, and they would make a good dinner. But they are all set out at once, to make the table groan and the guests sigh.

Deb's father, long gone, remains a presence with his hand-lettered labels, each with a delicate watercolour design, beside each dish—Korv, Limpa, Gurkor, Ost.

Heaping plates are emptied and filled again. Take some of every food to try.

Then go back for a bit of this, a spoonful of that, go around again.

Let time elapse, loosen the belts, talk with friends, play some music, then move on to the sweets. Pepperkakker, Spritz, Pfeffernusse . . . spicy, crisp or buttery, have one more . . . just one more.

I moved to Halifax, away from Deb, away from Smorgasbord down the road.

One year I tried very hard, coaxing, pleading, asking her to do it at a time of year, summer or fall, that involved no snow and no icy roads, so I could experience it one more time. It's a testament to how much work that dinner is that she absolutely refused. Nothing would budge her, not even the offer of a painting I knew she wanted.

So, I continue with my mouth-watering memories, as I serve my dish of pale green, crisp cucumbers.

Christmas Is Coming Up Fast

Lesley Crewe

Nowadays, when I think of the word Christmas, my mind automatically conjures up the warring factions in Facebook land.

We have the people who happily post a cartoon of Olaf, the snowman, belting out, "Only 300 days until Christmas!!!" and the rest of the population, screaming back, "NO! Say it ain't so!"

Christmas is an emotional time. Lots of holidays are special, but Christmas is the big enchilada.

It makes itself known the minute our Halloween pumpkins roll off the front porch. It's like a giant, pulsing machine, pushing us onward through November and gathering steam until we tear off that page in our calendars to reveal the big D: December.

Suddenly, as if realizing it for the first time, instead of every year of our lives, it hits us that we only have three weeks to get four years of work done by the 25th. That's three weeks and change!

How the heck did that happen?

Now, obviously, I'm looking at this from a tired, grownup woman's perspective, because tired grownup women are the ones, the general population somehow decided, who should shoulder the burden of this wondrous occasion. Possibly because this same population deemed that shopping, gift wrapping, cooking and decorating is something we women just love to do, on top of the other wondrous things we do in the run of a day, like working, and raising kids, and cleaning the house.

But I'm not going to leave men out of this equation. They, too, have their assigned duties at this time of year, risking life and limb to hang off a ladder and drape Christmas lights on rooftops and big trees in the front yard. They are also the ones stuck in the garage putting together bikes, train sets and dollhouses late into the night on Christmas Eve. It's also their lot in life to shovel the driveway, clean off the car and go collect Great-Grandad and his bulky wheelchair from the nursing home.

We moan about it endlessly, while we stand in store line-ups overheating in our winter jackets, and yet, like lemmings hurrying towards the edge of a cliff, we all fall willingly over the side.

We just have to. Because Christmas is the chance for us to be together again, and as our families grow and spread out across the globe, we desperately need an occasion to guilt the people we love into coming home to spend time with us.

And we honestly think that's what we want. Until we're in the middle of stuffing a turkey and an argument breaks out between eggnog swilling, long-time Conservative uncle Ernie and your die-hard Liberal auntie Joan, who's hopped up on her third gin and tonic.

Christmas is wonderful but messy. Kind of like life.

We have marvelous memories of being a kid, hanging up our stockings and leaving cookies and milk for Santa Claus and always a carrot for Rudolph. Of not being able to get to sleep, almost sick with excitement about opening presents in the morning. And then we have the not-so-great memories of the first time we couldn't get home for Christmas. Crying into our frozen dinner in a studio apartment far, far away, with our mom on the phone trying to make us feel better.

Or that first Christmas after you've lost someone. It's heart-breaking. You wish the whole day would just disappear and leave you alone. Everyone in the world is celebrating, except you.

Christmas can make happy people really happy, and sad

people really sad. Because it's a day, times a thousand. It's THE day.

Unfortunately, Christmas has become an industry of sorts. We now have whole weeks on television dedicated to Christmas movies, although why this is necessary, I'll never know. The script is the same every time. Savvy, gorgeous, determinedly-single business woman goes home for the holidays and bumps into the nerd from high school, who's now a gorgeous hunk who runs his own winery. Sparks fly during the town hall Christmas carolling contest. They fall into each other's arms while wearing ugly Christmas sweaters and kiss under the mistletoe. Fade to black.

But despite all the nonsense that threatens to drown Christmas in a commercialized quagmire, the simple reason we are all nostalgic for this time of year is the only reason that matters.

It's love.

Love for our family. Love for our friends and neighbours. Standing outside in the quiet of a winter's night, with snow falling gently around us. Wishing for peace on earth.

Christmas is "a thrill of hope, the weary world rejoices."

It's about a mouse named Jasper

Faith Farrell

Jasper was a contented creature if there ever was one. And if you were a contented Mouse in a house, there is no better time than the Winter holidays. Extra cheese all around, sugar cookie crumbs; an evergreen to be enjoyed indoors. Ribbon and string to make any mouse hole a home.

When the first of December rolled around, Jasper scurried to the kitchen expecting the boxes from the attic to already be cluttering the floor. But, there were no boxes. Not one to be found. How strange, he thought, December first was always the day that the boxes came down from the attic.

Usually music would be coming from the living room. Boughs of all varieties would be strewn all over the kitchen table, waiting to be garlanded together around doors and windows. The fresh smell of pine would be filling the room. Oranges would be drying in the oven. Popcorn would be overflowing bowls waiting to be strung. But, the kitchen was bare. Nary a note could be heard.

The old cookbook, stained and wrinkled, should have been down off the shelf waiting for its family secrets to be baked. But, it sat on the shelf collecting dust. There should have been peppermint sticks beside the coffee pot by now. But, not one.

And then Jasper remembered there was something very different about this first of December. This was the first December without the Old Woman. It had been her favourite time of year. It was she who would drag the boxes down from the attic. She who would put the music on.

Jasper had seen her get sick. He had worried for her. And then one day she was gone. The family had been dressed all in black. And even mice knew what that meant. The family had been grey ever since.

He had liked the Old Woman. She had always left him the best of crumbs. She'd leave all her best woven and woolly scraps out for his choosing. She had always shooed the cat away in a pinch. And every Christmas she never forgot him. He would wake to a generous square of cheese, always tied with a bow.

She wouldn't have liked this: A house stark and bare, empty of warmth, scents and music. She wouldn't have liked it. Not one little bit. The greyness, the moping, the family was struggling. It can be hard to learn how to go on. And even mice understood that. So maybe, Jasper thought, they just needed a little help.

He went to the living room and set about his work. He pulled from the desk a large stack of white paper and arranged it on the coffee table. He pulled the heavy scissors from the end table drawer, and the shaker of glitter. He retrieved the spool of fishing line and a roll of scotch tape from the junk drawer in the kitchen.

He took to folding and snipping. And when he was done, he unfolded his work. A snowflake perfectly formed. He made a few more and fanned them upon the table. An invitation for more. Then he went to the shelf and he pulled out a worn record. He flicked a switch with his tail and a familiar tune filled the room. Then he scurried away and he waited.

Slowly they came from all different corners of the house. They each had a smile, even if it was a bit sad. And they picked up the scissors and they cut up the paper snowflakes. Soon the room was filled with laughter and happy memories. None of them questioned it. Each thinking the other had started it. No one asked who, each just glad for a bright spot of merry.

No one suspected the Mouse who was hidden in the bookshelf. That night, Jasper went to bed with a smile on his whiskers, as paper snowflakes danced on strings from the ceiling. And so it went on. Each day something new. He kept up the spirit, it was the only thing to do.

One morning the mother and children woke to find the old recipe book on the counter, opened to their favourite cookie recipe. All the ingredients lined up and ready. So she and the children baked the day away. And she smiled to herself, how thoughtful her husband had been for setting it all up before he left for work. It was just the push she needed. Her heart felt a little lighter with a little Christmas cheer.

One evening the father came home from work to find the Christmas lights waiting to be put up. They had been dug from the garage, now resting in perfect coils, perfectly untangled. He breathed a sigh of relief. The Old Woman had been the one to untangle them every year. And if he was honest, he had been filled with dread of tackling, it without her. As he set up the ladder, he thought to himself how thoughtful his wife had been in taking the time to untangle them. It was just the push he needed. And he felt himself get a little bit lighter, a small spark of cheer in his heart.

One day the children were surprised to come home to Christmas cards spread on the kitchen table—everything that they needed to post a little cheer. Even some paper to write a letter or two to the North Pole. It had always been the Old Woman who sat with them, and helped them write. They didn't think anyone else had remembered. But here their parents had thought of everything, even the worn address book filled with the Old Woman's handwriting. They happily set about making a stack of merry mail. They thought it would make them miss her more. But what they found were happy memories welling up. And she felt a little closer. Their hearts were a little lighter, and they felt them warm.

Jasper's final act: the trimming of the tree. It took him all night to tote all their favourite ornaments down from the attic. He filled the coffee table with tinsel rope and hopeful strands of lights.

The tree itself was the trickiest of tricks. He brokered a deal with the squirrel from the front yard tree who swore to know a beaver from the river. As midnight approached, Jasper sat eagerly, if not a bit nervously, in the front room window. His eyes strained on the tree line. The cat sat beside him, her tail twitching in truce. In spite of her claws she was rooting for the little Mouse. Just when doubt started to creep in, there appeared Jasper's new flat-tailed friend of a friend. A backyard buck helped lean it up against the step.

And in the morning the family was surprised to find a tree waiting for them, seemingly delivered while they were all asleep. The Children assumed it had been their parents. The Mother thought it had been the Father, and Father the Mother. They were thankful, it was just the push they needed. They felt lighter, and set to the trimming. They turned on the music, and turned down the lights. And laughter filled the room from morning to night. Sometimes with tears, but they laughed just the same. Filled to the brim with memories of Christmases past.

Jasper retired to his home behind the bookcase. Decorating a small bough he had saved for himself. His heart was a little bit lighter. Their merriment spread.

Christmas Eve came and they feasted on turkey with all the trimmings, before they migrated to the living room. Jasper buffeted on all the best scraps as they exchanged gifts. Then he rolled himself back to the bookcase, hidden along the shelf, letting the warmth wrap around him. Maybe it was the merriment, or the warmth from the fire, or maybe it was his belly filled up to the brim—Jasper fell asleep nestled amongst the books.

When he awoke the room was quiet and dark, all except the twinkling lights of the tree. Jasper rubbed the sleep from his eyes, and then there He was. Carefully placing a gift beneath the tree. The rich, red velvet of his coat shimmering in the tree light. Then He walked across the room, his boots silent on the rug. He reached behind the chair that used to be the Old Woman's chair, and emerged with a knitting basket that had been forgotten to the dust.

From it he pulled two pairs of mittens, one hat and a thick pair of socks. And He placed each one carefully in the stockings that were hung. They were the last things the Old Woman had ever made. Then he turned to the bookcase, and Jasper didn't dare move. He walked right to him, and bent down on his knee. He reached in the basket and pulled out one last brightly colored little thing.

And in a deep whisper He said, "She would never forget you, Jasper." He gave him a smile that crinkled up by his eyes. "And neither will they." He gestured to the stockings on the mantle. "They may never know it was you. But they'll never forget the help you gave them on their first Christmas without her."

He gave Jasper a pat and a wink. And then He reached into his pocket and pulled out a square of cheese, with the neatest little bow that Jasper had ever seen. Just like that he was gone. Jasper's whiskers smiled at it all. He shed a happy, sad tear as he held the last gift from his dear friend against his chest. And he knew that all of this had been because she was missed.

Christmas Day came with the wonder of the family as they discovered the soon-to-be-cherished content of their stockings. They recognized the stitching. And they felt its warmth of love. The Children hugged their parents. And the Mother turned to the Father and said, "I don't know how you did it. These," she held up her socks, "the decorating, the baking, any of it." He gave her a puzzled wide-eyed look. He shook his head, "It wasn't me. I thought it was you!"

"If it wasn't you, then who was it?" the Children asked. They looked at each other with wonder. And they sat in bewilderment, with no answer but a shrug in their shoulders. Was it Santa? Or maybe their own Christmas Angel? But, there on the shelf sat hidden a Mouse, wearing a perfectly fit knit turtleneck that had been made just for him.

And he knew just like them, that Love was a gift that didn't end.

That it keeps and it grows in memories and hearts.

It's what makes a house a Home, as all contented Mice know.

Christmas ✦ ✦
New and Improved

Donna D'Amour

This Christmas will be better. I've made sure. I announced to the adult members of my family that I will not be exchanging gifts this year. I didn't want to be viewed as Scrooge, although I must admit that in the last few years, Christmas has been welcomed by a "Humbug!" from me. The frustration of finding just the right gift at just the wrong price, the hours of walking the malls in heavy winter clothing to check one more store, the mounting bills that hide behind the little plastic walls and pounce on you in the New Year, left me wondering. Peace on earth . . . get real.

I'd fallen into the commercial Christmas trap, obeying all three commandments:

• Thou shalt hold thy charge card high throughout this profitable season (early November to December 24).

• Thou shalt purchase a gift of equal or superior value to those gifts you received last year.

• Thou shalt take thy Christmas list each year, go forth and multiply.

It wasn't always like that. I remember when a gift was a small token of affection. As a child, I chose my wish list for the two-for-eighty-eight-cent page in the catalogue. My sisters and I were given one dollar to buy gifts for six other family members. Mom got little blue glass birds, Dad got his usual styptic pencil. (I didn't realize at the time that it would take a hemophiliac a lifetime to use up Dad's collection of styptic pencils.) I can't remember what the others received but I do know my sister Ann bought me a rag doll that year. It cost fifty cents, half of her Christmas money. I was overwhelmed by her generosity. I still am.

I must confess that I am tempted to pick up a little something for her. I even began a Christmas list. Andrea, my nine-year-old, looked over my shoulder.

"What does Uncle Allan look like?" she asked. "It's been so long since I've seen him, I forget."

I was stunned. She couldn't be serious. Why only last year he gave her a lovely microscope and, a year before, it was a pretty jogging suit. Suddenly it hit me. I take Christmas gifts to my mother's house a week before Christmas. I pick up the gifts from my brothers and sisters. Usually, I run into most of the family at that time. I hadn't noticed that in the past two years, I'd just missed my brother and his wife. The presents were exchanged but no meeting took place. The gifts were no longer a token of affection—they were a substitute.

That discovery gave me the courage to call a halt to it all. I tried to tell Andrea what Christmas used to be like. I tried to describe Uncle Allan's entertaining the family with his stories. I tried to describe his deep husky laugh and his important place in the family, but I couldn't quite capture it . . . .

You had to be there.

So, this Christmas will be different. I didn't get any opposition from my family. A few said they had wanted to put an end to it years ago but were afraid to hurt anyone's feelings. I'll still buy for the children and for Grandma, but these gifts are fun and an expression of love.

I'll visit with family. Both my daughters will get acquainted with relatives they seldom see throughout the year. They will take away a memory of a Christmas shared, a tale or two to carry on to future years, a smile from a proud aunt, a wink from a happy Grandma, a hug from a tiny cousin, a sense of belonging.

I'll save my tokens for the tollbooth. This year I will opt for affection, straight out. Definitely a new and improved celebration.

That Crooked Little Grin

Steve Woods

Does it seem to you that magical things happen more often around Christmas time? It sure does seem that way to me. This story is proof of that.

It was September 1972, and I was about to start Grade Twelve in Sydney Mines High, my first year as a student there.

My family in Montreal had broken up, and I elected to live with my grandfather in Sydney Mines, in an area known as "Cranberry." Our house in Cranberry was about an hour's walk from the school, and there were no school buses for high school students at the time. Also, there was no cafeteria in Sydney Mines High, so the school shut down for lunch from 12 noon until 1:30 pm. During that time, one had to leave the school and find a way home and back, or find a place to "brown-bag" it.

The only public transportation in Sydney Mines at the time was the Allen Bus Company, which left the pit yard at Princess Colliery in Cranberry precisely on the hour, taking miners home after their shift. Getting to the pit yard was at least a fifteen-minute brisk walk from where we lived as well, and if I was late for the bus I would have to walk to school, missing the first period. So I made sure, as best I could, that I wouldn't be late for the bus.

Unfortunately, the morning bus left the pit yard at nine—exactly the same time as the first class started. Every morning I was ten to fifteen minutes late for class. I tried to explain my dilemma to the principal and my homeroom teacher, but they were unsympathetic and told me that I was supposed to be, and expected to be, at school at nine.

I would jump off the bus in front of the Red Brick Row across from the high school on Main Street in Sydney Mines and run as if the devil himself was chasing me across the street, trying to get to class as soon as I could. But when I entered the class, every morning almost without fail, the teacher's comment that greeted me would be the same: "Now that the Cranberry contingent has decided to grace us with his presence, perhaps we can begin our lesson." Being basically shy, I wanted to blend in, not stick out like an annoying sore thumb.

In our classes, the desks were the type that sat two students side by side; the fellow next to me was an affable fellow named Pat, who lived closer to the school and managed to get there on time every morning. He had sympathy for me and understood that for the most part the situation was out of my control unless I was lucky enough to catch a ride with someone going to town.

So, I decided to try to fix things; I would get my own transportation.

With only $250 to my name I knew it wasn't going to be easy, but I began searching for something, anything, that I could drive to school. I found a British 1965 MG 1100 "Saloon." Not at all like its sporty MGB cousins, this little oddball of a car looked like a rusty box of Kleenex with a roof and a windshield, nestled on wheels. It had problems, but I had worked on my mother's 1960 Austin Mini in Montreal.

So, for $150 it was mine, and I proudly showed it to my grandfather as if it were a Ferrari. He squinted at it through a veil of smoke from his hand-rolled cigarette, laughed a bit, then without saying a word he patted me on the shoulder, turned and went back into the house. But with constant effort in a mechanical sense to keep it running, it got me back and forth to school.

The "Cranberry Contingent" wasn't going to be late anymore.

Along came the week before Christmas break, and many students had flown the coop early, leaving the classrooms almost half empty. The teacher told us that the students from 12C class would be joining us, as their class was empty too. Students began filing into our classroom, sitting in the vacant seats.

Then, she walked through the door.

She was slightly taller than the girls with her, engaged in conversation, smiling and laughing as she clutched her books to her chest.

She was stunning, and I had trouble not staring at her.

Pat said to me, "That's Mary."

Pat talked too loudly. Mary turned, and looked at us, then fixed her gaze on me. Then it happened. She gave me this cute crooked little grin, and I just about melted.

She then turned around, put her left elbow on the desk and rested her cheek on it, as she began writing. Her right leg was jutting out slightly behind the desk—a visage forever burned into my memory.

Christmas break 1972—I spent quality time with my grandfather. But the image of that girl had planted itself into a little corner of my head. I didn't see her often around the halls of the school. Eventually, scholastic life returned to normal.

It was around the middle of January, Christmas had come and gone, and life returned to what was ordinary, at least as ordinary as life could be at the time. About halfway through last period, a girl in my class named Debra approached me and said, "Steve, you're the guy with that little car? I wonder if you could do my friend a favour? She needs a drive home." "Yeah, tell her not to lollygag, the little car tends to fill up in a hurry."

When I went to get in the car there were already three youngsters in the back seat from the elementary school down the road. Then the passenger door opened, and she got in.

The Crooked Little Grin Girl.

The lump in my throat felt like a golf ball. But I managed a "sure." I turned the ignition key and with a grinding noise, gnashing of gears and a puff of blue smoke, we were off.

I did an illegal u-turn. And my mind was racing: "What should I say to her? I have to say something! If I don't say anything, she'll think I'm weird! But if I say the wrong thing, she'll KNOW I'm weird. What to do? What to do?"

"So, Mary, what are your plans for after graduation?"

She looked at me, flashed that crooked little grin, and said, "I'm going to become a mortician."

Well, I managed somehow to bring the little car to a stop, and sat there for about ten seconds, gathering my thoughts. I looked at her again, and she was still wearing that crooked little grin.

She jumped out, smiled and said, "Thanks!" Needless to say, the rest of the day was mostly a blur.

After high school, life got busier. Jobs here and there, community college, started working in the mine, got married. Day-to-day life has a way of chewing up time, and the years flew past. Eventually, as often happens when people get married too young, my marriage ended, and I found myself living a single life again. It was an adjustment, after thirty-five years.

Never a party animal, nor a social butterfly, my pastime when not working was to go to Tim's, get a coffee and sit alone doing the Soduku and Crossword puzzles. One day, I was interrupted by a person saying, "Steve? Steve, from Sydney Mines? Is that you?" It was Debra, from Sydney Mines High. She was meeting a friend in the food court for a coffee. "Her name is Mary, she lived up on Forest Street."

The Crooked Little Grin girl? No way.

And there she was, Mary. So, I let her pass by me, about 10 paces, and said in a muted tone, "Mary?"

She stopped and turned around. And then it happened.

That Crooked Little Grin.

All the high school memories, each and every one, came rushing back like a tidal wave.

We sat in the food court, and I listened to her relate how her life had unfolded; she had moved to Alberta after graduation, married, and had six children. Her husband had passed away several years before. With six mouths to feed, she started working as an operator in the oil fields, the first female for that huge oil company. I was impressed. She didn't just break the "glass ceiling," she demolished it.

She wasn't in town long, just to help her mother convalesce. But we stayed in touch, and texts turned into emails which turned into phone calls which turned into video chats; then one day she said, "You're off for Christmas. Why don't you come out to Alberta for a visit, and I'll show you around a bit?"

"Some things never change."

I realized that I was falling deeply in love with this wonderful lady and her grin and thought to myself that I couldn't, wouldn't have it any other way.

Then, it was my turn! She came to visit me, and the times were good indeed. By then I had a much more reliable vehicle, and we did some traveling around Cape Breton. I asked her if she remembered me driving her home on that day so long ago, and remarkably she said that she did.

Then I asked her about the mortician thing, and she explained, "I liked you, and was just teasing." I told her that she had almost given me a heart attack, to which she laughed out loud.

Shortly after, I noticed that we were approaching the very same street corner where long ago she had told me that she was going to become a mortician. "So, Mary, what are your plans?"

She paused slightly, looked at me; gave me that irresistible crooked little grin, and said, "I think I'm going to marry you."

Christmas came early that year, because that's exactly what she did.

Root Beer for Christmas

David Early

In the days when I lived according to the *Whole Earth Cata-logue* and *Mother Earth News* and *Organic Gardening*, I found a recipe for making beer at home. The initial equipment was fairly reasonable to locate and buy, and once that re-useable equipment was working for me, I figured my winter's beer should be had at a terrific savings. My wife didn't drink beer—she'd prefer wine— and looking back, I don't think I was much of a drinker. But for some reason I decided to stock up, and this was my first brewing adventure. And my last.

As a fellow told me once, nothing wrong with making an alcoholic drink. All it took was a few ingredients you'd likely find around the house. But as I remember, he was talking about moonshine, and an additional illegal run.

As it happened, my dream fell apart at the moment that might be called "greed." The recipe called for about half a teaspoon of sugar into each bottle right before it was capped. And I figured if half a teaspoon was good then likely a full teaspoon would make the drink that much stronger, that much better.

I prepared and capped four boxes of the old Canadian stub bottles, each with about a teaspoon of sugar. Then I put the boxes in a cool, dark place in the cupboard under the stairs—to finish brewing.

I don't remember how long it took—possibly the first night, maybe the second. But we were in bed, the fire was banked and we were sleeping—when I woke up to the first loud snap like a gunshot. I prowled the house after another loud pop or two, and realized that bottles were exploding behind the cupboard door, under the stairs.

I stood at the closed door and listened to the erratic bang, bang . . . bang! Then a long silence. Then Bang! And I knew I wasn't going to open that door for the rest of that night.

The next morning, there was the occasional exploding bottle.

Finally, I dressed for winter—wool cap, heavy coat and mitts, just about every part of me covered. Holding a thick blanket high and open as a shield, I slowly opened the door under the stairs. Then I moved in and covered the boxes with the thick blanket.

Then, carefully using another blanket, I moved under the first one and picked up one box wrapped in a blanket. I worked my way through the house to the back yard and put the box on the ground. Then I started throwing good-sized rocks at the blanket-covered box, listening for the break of glass. One after another, I brought out the four boxes and stoned them.

I probably left the boxes and blankets out there for a week. No more bottles burst. Possibly I had broken all the rest. I uncovered a box at a time and with a long pole I broke any survivors. Now all I had to do was safely clean up the glass.

Christmas came and anything alcoholic was a gift or a purchase from the liquor store. I knew the cause of my failure but now the heart had gone out of it. I bought and served root beer for that year's holiday.

Our Sneaky Christmas

Lena Mahoney-Petrie

"I'll quit! There's no way I'll miss another holiday with my family."

These words were uttered with a mixture of frustration and anger by my husband Jim. He meant it. An email sent to workers with the December schedule demanded a return to work back to the oil patch on Christmas Day. It was not received well by the workers. Christmas suddenly became a balance sheet for the benefit versus personal loss of the long-distance life we were living. I knew some creative solutions were going to be needed for the approaching holidays.

In the 2000s, the Oil Patch in our Canadian western province was heavily engaged in developing the Canadian oil industry. The booming Oil Patch was such a massive scale development there arose a large demand for workers of skilled trades from across Canada. Most particularly sought after were "East Coast" workers from Nova Scotia, Newfoundland and Labrador, New Brunswick, and Prince Edward Island. Known for their strong work ethic, adaptability and tenacity, east coast workers were highly recruited by competing oil and trade companies. If you worked in trades or the service industry and were willing to commit to the challenges and sacrifices that working "out west" required, there were great career opportunities. Places like Cape Breton, Nova Scotia, had been in a downturn and enduring a mass exodus off the island in the recent decade from the closing of prime resource industries of coal and steel, and cod fishing. Working out west became a godsend for families to keep their homes and continue living in Cape Breton. The downside was that it was a four-thousand-kilometre commute away from home for weeks at a time. Everyone you knew had at least one family member working and commuting to work out west which became a way of life here in Cape Breton.

The possibility of Jim, my husband, who had worked out west for six years, throwing away his job for one day—Christmas Day—was an emotional response and not a rational one, born of too many lost days that were part of the price of doing his work away from his family. The reality of leaving family behind at home and living "in camp" was a hardship that can only truly be known by those who experienced it. Just as important and at times challenging was the role of the caregiver left home to manage the family and household on their own. Spouses and partners endured this for the sake of their families—so we needed to come up with a plan to save our Christmas.

As I pondered the scheduling issue for Jim's return to work date being on Christmas Day, I began to entertain a sneaky idea that might work for our family. What if Christmas Day wasn't celebrated on the 25th of December? What if we could celebrate one day earlier on the 24th of December? It would seem as if Dad (my husband Jim) was home for Christmas and returned to work after Christmas, on what we would call Boxing Day—and it would not be so hard on the family to have the real Chrstmas Day without him. For me, Christmas was about family and the traditions we practiced; the date we celebrated really did not matter.

Before I brought the idea to my husband, I reached out to Santa, explaining that celebrating one day ahead of schedule was needed for a happy Christmas for our children and for Jim and, therefore, for me. Once I explained my plan in my letter, Santa was okay with the plan. Then I told Jim the details.

Like me, Jim had learned to love the holidays after the children were born. There was nowhere on the planet he would rather be than home with us. Our home was a warm and cozy three-bedroom bungalow on three acres on the outskirts of Sydney, in a rural farming community which had been transitioning slowly to suburban mix. It still gave neighborhood children the opportunity to grow up and move like a small herd, with fields for cross-country skiing, skating on quarries, and forest adventures in the summers. We had had great fun preparing carrots and water for the reindeer, left where we knew the reindeer and sleigh would park. Our own eyes had seen the hoof prints and sleigh tracks in the snow and on our roof!

I assured Jim that our son John would be cool about Santa.

John was a twelve-year-old and a gentle giant of a boy with blond hair and big blue eyes and a huge generous heart who loved his family. We watched his face fall when we told him that his dad had to go back to work on Christmas Day this year. We told John that we had cleared it with Santa to have our Christmas one day early and make the next day feel like Boxing Day. We all agreed that that would be better than having Dad leave on Christmas Day.

John thought for a moment. He said, "Lauren will never believe it's Christmas Day early . . . she will know the difference."

Lauren at nine years old was our witty, tall, strong daughter with strawberry brown hair who looked older than her years, but was still excited about what Santa might bring Christmas Morning.

I continued telling Jim how this could work. It meant reaching out to the parents of the children's friends, sharing our sneaky plan for those couple of days. Neighbours understood and agreed to distract their kids from wanting to visit on the days close to Christmas.

John loved his little sister and knew her well. He understood how excited Lauren was for Santa and didn't want her surprise ruined, but he needed more convincing. We told him, "There is one thing that will convince her: You have to change the date on the computer. Do you think you can do this; can you keep this secret?" John nodded his commitment to the plan.

To start our sneaky Christmas, I mentioned something at supper—because tomorrow would be the 23rd, which would become our Christmas Eve.

After supper, still at the table, I casually asked the kids what they needed for decorating their cookies tomorrow night as I was planning on grocery shopping early the next morning before the stores got crowded on Christmas Eve. At first Lauren didn't pay any attention to what I had just said but then suddenly whipped her head around stating, "Tomorrow? Wait, what . . . tomorrow isn't Christmas Eve." I looked at her and gave a bit of a grin and said, "Yes, it is." "No, it's not . . . tomorrow is NOT Christmas Eve!" Lauren looked confused and concerned. "We just got off school. Tomorrow is not Christmas Eve!"

John played his part brilliantly, laughing at Lauren and saying, "Okay little sis," reaching out to pat her head, which gesture she particularly minded receiving from her big brother. Jim added a bit of teasing by saying, "Well okay, if you don't believe us, you don't have to open a present with us tomorrow night." Lauren jumped up with a determined look on her face and ran to the computer. We could hear her saying, "Wow. We just got off school. That time sure went by fast." As she came back into the kitchen, John smiled in perfect, big brother behaviour. Lauren was reluctantly convinced that tomorrow was Christmas Eve.

In our family there are many traditions that we enjoy. Some originated from my husband's family, the Petries, and some from my Mahoneys family, and others born from our own family. Christmas Eve meant a special supper with pies: meat pie, green tomato mincemeat, and apple for Jim. Then just one present was opened, and Christmas-cookie-making followed.

The children were always excited despite they knew that the one present opened on Christmas Eve would be new red pyjamas and a small treat, but they were still appreciative to get immediately into new cozy pj's and start the cookie-making. I had the extra dough ready from the shortbread batch. They used all sorts of shapes of cookie cutters: socks, stars, candy canes, Santa and reindeer with coloured sprinkles, nuts, smarties, coconut. And then icing after they were baked and cooled. Each cookie was original and a beautiful baked piece of art.

After the cookies and milk were prepared on Santa's own plate and the reindeer food left outside, our family settled into watching holiday movies such as *A Christmas Story*, *Rudolf*, or *Mr. Bean's Xmas*. Trying to get children to sleep on this "Christmas Eve" took some time. While Jim and I waited to put the family presents under the tree, we lounged in our new pj's and enjoyed a Christmas bevy such as rum and eggnog and Christmas beer. That means regular beer enjoyed at Christmas time while watching *Trailer Park Boys Christmas Special.*

Waking up Christmas morning no matter what age, or in our case no matter what date, always gives that feeling of surprise and thrill. An instant catch of breath realizing that it's Christmas morning! For our family, it meant being roused by our children around 7:00 a.m. with a raucous knocking and bounding through our bedroom door. "Mama, Mama, Da, Da . . . it's Christmas; wake up, wake up, come on, get up!" We made our way to the living room and what a sight it was to see. Such an assortment of pretty red and green paper, gold, silver and white bows covered the waiting presents. Near the woodstove were stockings for everyone, even Dashy the cat, and we opened them before a special Christmas breakfast of Scotch eggs, white pudding and pancakes.

Lauren suddenly remembered Santa's plate. "Santa drank most of the milk and the cookies are gone." Jim reminded her to look out the window, "Check the carrots and water." "Tracks! . . . I see sleigh tracks, and there are just bits of carrots left. The reindeer must have eaten them!" Then, after breakfast, Mom and Dad with coffees in hand, and children jumping with excitement, headed into the living room and gathered around our real fir tree that smelled so good, shining with lights and many hand-made ornaments created by the children. And so began the most exciting part of Christmas, the opening of the presents.

We wore our red, fur-trimmed Christmas hats. Jim's was a plaid hunting hat with reindeer antlers that played music. He struggled to keep it on his head while he passed out the presents one at a time. We took lots of pictures and videos to look back on, as Christmas mornings become the indelible memories that remain in our minds and hearts from our childhood. That year was counted among one of the most memorable.

The day after our sneaky Christmas, our Boxing Day, really December 25th, was Jim's fly-out day. We had a relaxing quiet morning, enjoyed a great brunch from an abundance of rich leftovers. The children were engaged with their games and presents while Jim began packing to return to work. We would need to drive Jim to the airport for his flight to Halifax, then to Toronto and on to Fort McMurray. We had learned long ago that waiting at the airport only prolonged the difficulty of leaving. We would say goodbye in the parking lot and let him go and let him let us go, for another while. The goodbye's that day were hard. Hugging me, Jim whispered. "We pulled it off, I think . . . ." I smiled "Yes," and then drove away with a wave goodbye.

The drive home was quiet; the children busied themselves on new games. We decided to take a drive through Sydney to see the Christmas lights on the houses. A favourite house to view every year was the spectacular Mombourquette home on Churchill Drive. On Kings Road, as I approached the intersection of Churchill and Kings, waiting for the traffic light, I noticed the large "Welcome to Membertou" sign. There was the digital message running across the large screen: "Temperature . . . 0 degrees Celsius . . . Time . . . 6:35 pm . . . Date . . . December 25, 2012 . . . MERRY CHRISTMAS." I gasped. December 25!

Lauren looked up from her game. The light was still red. "Look, look over there," I spouted excitedly. "Down there at that apartment building . . . look at all the lights down there." The kids agreed politely, the traffic light turned green and I rounded corner at such a speed, we were almost on two wheels.

The shining extensive display up on the street was beautiful and festive; the magic of the lights distracted us from returning home, just the three of us.

Later at bed time, I hugged John and told him we had pulled off our sneaky family Christmas. It would be another ten years before we shared this information with Lauren. There was no way Jim would go away on Christmas Day . . . and, because of our sneaky Christmas, he didn't have to.

Lessons of Life and Leadership from the Real Saint Nicholas

Tom Urbaniak

Saint Nicholas, the historical and humble Bishop of Myra (in present-day Turkey), put individual people before systems, before ideologies, and before arguments about doctrine and politics.

This Christmas, I am reflecting on what we can learn—what I can learn—from the way in which the actual Saint Nicholas went about his difficult work and hard life. Can his example somehow help me to be a better community person?

Nicholas was born around the year 270. None of his writings have survived. But his ministry produced extensive oral testimonies in disparate locations. People—not just Christians—loved this gentle soul. Many of these passed-down memories were later recorded or interpreted in writing.

Some of the tomes, such as *The Life of Saint Nicholas*, written by Michael the Archimandrite in the ninth century, were "hagiographies." In other words, they were specifically intended to idealize the person and thus inspire readers.

But in recent years there has been solid academic scholarship on the life of Nicholas. I particularly enjoyed Prof. Adam English's book *The Saint Who Would Be Santa Claus: The True Life and Trials of Nicholas of Myra*.

When Nicholas was born, there were only about two million Christians in the world. They usually met in private homes, and the act of gathering together was important to them. Their bishops were mostly not ladder-climbing mini-princes wearing expensive rings, but courageous guides, travellers (slogging through physical pain, which Nicholas himself experienced), and spiritual healers. They were usually selected by the priests or laity of their region.

Nicholas was not a convert. Both of his parents, who likely died during an epidemic when Nicholas was a teenager, are thought to have already been Christians.

The Christian community was known for doing good deeds for strangers and for identifying with the poor and weak. Although the Christians had their disputes about how to understand the Gospels, and disagreed on who was really in communion with them, they were not yet weighed down with volumes of canon law, palatial real estate, many layers of hierarchy, and cold church bureaucracies.

The core teachings of Jesus were still fresh for them: Love one another. Love your enemies. God loves everyone. Side with the weak. Don't get corrupted by ambition and power. Be true to the holy light within you. Be joyful in the face of adversity. Form communities to serve.

This was still before the Emperor Constantine embraced Christianity. That happened in the year 312—during the life of Nicholas—and dramatically changed power dynamics in many places, sometimes corrupting the Christian leaders.

It seems that Nicholas had spent time in jail for his beliefs and teachings. But as power shifted in the Christians' favour, his head did not swell. His leadership was still personal. His approach was still about taking risks to extend love and perform good deeds.

For Nicholas, no person was expendable or disposable.

In places where Nicholas ministered, infanticide—killing newborn babies or toddlers—was not precluded by law. Nor was selling daughters into sexual slavery. Women were sometimes killed with total impunity. Nicholas was reported to have raised money to purchase the rescue of victims, intending to pay anonymously.

From the sources, it is also quite likely he intervened for mistreated prisoners and denounced bribed judges who were willing to unjustly condemn people. He pleaded with generals to stop looting. He befriended foreign sailors, fed them and prayed with them before perilous journeys.

Most of the time, there would be no reward for him. He knew he would never see the people again.

Sources are divided on whether Nicholas was at the famous First Council of Nicaea (year 325). The Council was held to resolve doctrinal disputes on such questions as the relationship of Jesus to the Father. Although there are a few accounts of Nicholas getting into some kind of fight at the Council, it's more likely that he was a minor player among the two hundred or more bishops who were there.

Indeed, I would not be surprised if Nicholas glazed over the finer points. His worldview seemed to be more about justice through solidarity with others than it was about insisting on dogma.

In our time and place, I hope for the "Nicholas way": love and kindness without expectation of return; love and kindness even after we have been hurt in some way.

And may I have the courage to not look the other way when someone is forgotten or mistreated.

Mincemeat Pies and the Doot Doot

Gerald French

When I was six years old, growing up on Cape Breton Island in Sydney, I wondered about two things as Christmas approached: What presents would I ask Santa to bring, and what kind of meat was in mincemeat pie? Was it rabbit, moose or magical elf meat? My earliest holiday memories were the smell of spruce branches in our front porch and my Dad pulling me around the neighborhood through the snow on my little wooden sled. And of course, my big sister Sharon stealing my Mom's beer and drinking it with friends. She refilled the bottles with apple juice. Obviously, my Mom discovered the old switcheroo.

My Dad always started Christmas preparations very early. He was responsible for getting the stocking stuffers. He would always pick a day in August and announce to my Mom, "Marie, I'm going shopping for gifts for the Christmas stockings!" He was like James Bond on a secret mission. At the end of the day, he would return like a triumphant war veteran. "The stocking stuffers are done!" The bags of merchandise would disappear into my parents' bedroom closet until Christmas Eve.

At 6:00 a.m. on Christmas morning, I rushed downstairs to the living room. My mother joined me ten minutes later. Dad was a night owl kind of guy so he slept a few hours longer. Sharon was also still sleeping. I felt euphoric as I opened my presents. But I was not as enthusiastic when my mom turned on the record player and Wilf Carter began yodelling "Silver Bells . . . Yoalady

39

Hoo!" My mom sat beside me and opened a few of her presents. She already knew what was in them. Mom snuck under the tree a few days before Christmas Day. She would rip tiny holes in the wrapping paper to peek at her gifts. She hated surprises so she peeked every year. My Dad would laugh. "A little mouse was nibbling at your presents, Marie!"

I tore wrapping paper and unveiled my presents from jolly St Nick: a toboggan, a GI Joe action figure who talked when you pulled his dog tags, and a tabletop hockey game! Then I spotted a Sherwood hockey stick under the tree with my name on a tag. I ran around the house pretending I was Guy Lafleur. But I tripped on a piece of carpet and jabbed myself in the stomach with the stick, knocking the wind out of me. When I recovered minutes later from the high sticking incident, I thought it was a good time to investigate my Christmas stocking. Mom had painted the grey fireplace bricks red and put a big white letter F near the top. The F was either for our family name "French" or "Fireplace." I never asked.

The stockings were laid out on the floor. They were not hung up on the mantel. They were probably too heavy to stay up there. I felt like Indiana Jones discovering a secret cave. I dived on the floor and pulled items from my green and red stocking. There was a new *Hockey Illustrated* magazine, an orange, Santa-shaped chocolates, and soap on a rope that looked just like a baseball! I was a lucky boy.

After pulling out a tiny scented candle that displayed a message when it burned to the bottom, I felt a familiar shape in the sock. There was a Laura Secord chocolate hockey puck—my personal favorite. (A few years later I found a real rubber puck in my stocking and almost bit into it.) Then I grabbed the next sock item. It was a small white cardboard tube. "Dad, what's this?"

"It's a doot doot," he replied.

"What does it do?" I asked.

His eyes twinkled behind his thick pop-bottle-like glasses

with black frames. He reached out and placed the tube up to his lips. Then he yelled into it, "Doot doot!"

My mom, Sharon and I laughed. And from then on, we received doot doots in our stockings every year. My dad had a tremendous sense of humour but I wondered if he wore his steel plant safety helmet a little too tight!

It is now forty years later and I'm in charge of the stocking stuffers for my family. I always include a doot doot in my little girl's stocking. And she groans and laughs, "Oh Dad!" Our daughter has also provided some humour at Christmas time. On Christmas morning one year, she looked at the presents under the tree. "Holy sticks! Who's going to clean up all this?" When she was four, Genevieve sat on Santa's lap and pointed out the bells on his boots. "Santa, please don't wake me when you come to my house. Your boots are noisy!"

We visited Santa at the Bedford Place Mall two years later. Our six-year-old daughter confessed, "Santa, I just want a picture of Jesus for Christmas."

Santa looked over at me as if to say, "Is this girl kidding me?" No Santa, she is not.

Genevieve did add a few more gift ideas before Christmas. Meanwhile, I searched for a mincemeat pie recipe. Some of them do have pork or beef. Other mincemeat pies do not. My mom's mincemeat pie contained dates, figs, apples and raisins. I was always more of a blueberry or cherry pie fan.

I now know all of these Christmas memories are the best gifts that I received. Especially the love and laughter. It's not what's under my tree that matters. It's who is around it.

Ev's Pinwheels

Brenda Sampson

Our beautiful mother Evelyn nourished the world in so many ways. Food was one of the many ways she showed love, and she was good at it. People raved about her incredible meals and baked goods, and she made Christmastime special by hosting meals in our dining room and sharing her Lebanese food learned from my grandmother Josie, and from her mom Sal's recipes.

Sal's unique mac-and-cheese with tomatoes was so popular that my uncles used to ask her, "Please, Mom, make it in the bathtub!"

Mom's family used to own and run the Sally Ann Bakery in Glace Bay, and Mom baked beautifully. From the age of four, I was fortunate to grow up baking at her side and learning her craft and all of her baking "tips and tricks."

We grew up in Westmount/Edwardsville on the Canadian Coast Guard College grounds, where Dad was a civilian instructor. It was the best playground in the world—a place where we rode our bikes with the local kids, and we played road hockey, soccer and baseball until it was dark and we had to come in.

We had the best of all worlds: our grandparents and family in North Sydney and Glace Bay, our school friends in Edwardsville and Westmount, and our international community at the college. What a wonderful world it was—playing with children from all over the world: France, England, Chile, India, Edwardsville, of course—you name it!

Ev's Pinwheels

Our Christmases kicked off with a children's party at the grand, beautifully decorated Officer's Mess. Breathlessly, we waited for Santa to arrive on the fire truck in his bright red outfit with a sprig of holly on his hat. The challenge was: Who could get a glimpse of him first—all yelling, "I see him, I see him!"

There was a bag of candy and a small thoughtful gift for each child, and a huge potluck "spread" with delicious traditional food from all over the world made by each family on the Coast Guard base. For us, it was a bigger deal than Disneyland!

Mom always made peanut butter and banana pinwheel finger sandwiches for the party, and they were like a small miracle to us. She patiently cut the crusts off sandwich bread, spread peanut butter on the slices and carefully placed sliced banana on them. Then she guided them around each other one by one to make a log. After being wrapped in wax paper and chilled in the fridge, Mom would slice them like a jellyroll. Voila, beautiful pinwheel finger sandwiches, a Christmas delicacy and a work of art—a tantalizing, tasty treat!

We had so much to choose from with the delicious food on the huge table, so what did we do? My little brothers, Mark and Carl, would be searching, searching, and we all wondered . . . where were Mom's pinwheels?

While we later enjoyed some of the other lovely international treats, Ev's pinwheels were always our first choice. She made many wonderful snacks, dips, baked good and dishes for the holidays—including the traditional turkey dinner with the best gravy you ever tasted, tortière (Acadian meat pie), chicken pot pie, Lebanese cabbage rolls, kibbah, Syrian soup, lasagna, epic homemade rolls, fruitcake, squares, pies and cookies.

Yet for us, Ev's pinwheels kicked off the holiday season. They were the taste of Christmas!

Christmas on the *Cape Norman*

Albert Miles

I was the galley cook on the fishing draeger *Cape Norman* under Captain Gerald Vallis, working for National Sea Products, leaving Louisbourg to fish the Grand Banks off Newfoundland for ten days at a go—and to return with a hold full of cod, haddock, halibut, and other fish.

Before we left Louisbourg, I would place an eight-thousand-dollar grocery order at one of the stores in town, enough to do us for the whole ten days.

I had a big galley where I fixed the meals for the crew. I had a nice-sized room with a nice-sized bunk off the galley.

We had a good bunch of crew, and if I wasn't in the galley cooking, I'd be out on deck helping the crews to haul in the net, gut the fish, and put the catch down in the hold and ice them off.

The draeger had one big net with two big wooden doors at the front with a lead pipe under the doors to belly the net down to the floor of the ocean. There were also rollers on the bottom of the net. After two hours of dragging the net across the sea bottom, we would haul it up on deck and open it to release the catch on deck. The gear went back over the side. Then, for two hours, all the crew would gut the fish, ice off the catch, and put it down in the hold.

We never celebrated Christmas on the draeger—there was no Christmas gear on board. Christmas started when we hit the dock. Then we would buy our presents before we headed home.

This one December, I remember it being so stormy—high winds and high waves. The draeger would climb a tall wave and suddenly drop over the top so you could see the propellers turning above the water. And coming down the slope of the wave, the draeger would pull over and tip to one side.

Despite all that, we made it back to Louisbourg for Christmas.

I remember seeing all the colours of the Christmas lights in the windows of the houses around Louisbourg Harbour.

I had already cleared and cleaned the galley and stowed all my pots and pans. The rest of the crew cleared up outside, so everything was put away before we reached the dock.

All the crew hurried home for Christmas with their families—some of them as far away as Newfoundland. A lot of them hurried off to get drunk.

I would get a taxi to North Sydney and enjoy a big turkey dinner with my sister, Kathleen—or "Kay" as we all called her—and her two girls and three boys. I had a big family all over the place.

As for presents, one of the things I gave was fresh cod, haddock, and halibut steaks. Everybody loves eating fish over the holidays.

After the New Year, I would get another big grocery order and fill my galley with enough food for ten days out on the ocean.

The crew returned from their holiday, and the *Cape Norman* set out from Louisbourg to the Grand Banks for another ten days of fishing.

Yet Another Story About Childhood Innocence

Nancy Smith

There is a renowned author and storyteller who lives fairly close to me, and if there is one thing I have learned from him, it is to set the stage. Bare facts are not enough for a story. So, first I am hoping to set the stage:

Another winter has passed, and the conversations commonly heard for the past few months would go somewhat like this: "Snow in the forecast for tomorrow!"; "Had to shovel today"; "Waiting to have my driveway plowed"; "Anyone see the salt truck go through?" and "After that mild spell it is all ice under foot."

While chitchatting with friends of my vintage, I began to reflect on my younger days growing up in a rural Cape Breton community. This particular snapshot in time happened in the mid-Fifties. That would be the days prior to colour TV, with no internet or Facebook and, for some, no indoor plumbing. The man in the moon only meant one thing—no man ON the moon!

Winter began by the end of October, and it was not unusual to wear our snowsuits under our Halloween costumes—which were homemade and very simple, made from whatever we could find. The occasion wasn't solely about the treats. It was about the carefree get-together with neighbours and friends. Our two feet were our mode of transportation; someone driving us from house to house—what?! No treats were tampered with and very few were store-bought. You couldn't wait to knock on the door of certain homes because there you would get the best-ever fudge or molasses candy or cookies. Oh yeah, the good old days!

When December came around there were tons of snow and cold—bitter cold, sometimes. The high drifts with packed snow made a good basis for tunnels, underground dwellings, and forts, accompanied by snowball fights. The creations were only limited by your imagination. The tunnels and underground apartments—yeah, that could have been dangerous if the ceilings collapsed, but they didn't. I guess these were our version of playing in the traffic. We lived to see another day!

When dusk fell the door of the house would open and someone would call, usually our Mother, "Supper is ready!" We would come in to the cozy warmth of a wood stove, our cheeks would be beet red, snot would be running from our nostrils (at times half frozen), and we would be hungry as all get-out.

There was one memorable Christmas Eve that has stayed with me for so many years. At this time in our lives our family lived in a modest bungalow-style home. At the back of the house there was a ladder up to the roof. I cannot ever remember that ladder not being there. Oh yes, lots of snow on the roof. Santa was coming tonight at last, after our months of anticipation. We quickly readied ourselves for bed. We were all revved up for the visit from the old guy from the north, along with his mode of transportation—a sleigh propelled by eight deerpower.

Although our bodies were weary our minds were exploding with excitement. We were giggly, oh so giggly. We were told a number of times to settle down and go to sleep. The sleep didn't come but the giggles kept coming. Finally, our Dad came into the room and said, "You'd better get to sleep because I hear Santa Claus is up near Neil R's!" Well that did it—asleep we went.

Morning came and yes, our stockings were filled—modest by today's standards but they held more value than a warehouse full of electronic gadgets. Once we settled down, our Dad told us to put on our jackets and boots, he had something to show us. He led us to the back of the house, to the aforementioned ladder. There it was—sleigh tracks in snow on the roof!

Man, the day couldn't get any better! Santa was really, really here! If ever there was a WOW moment in my life, that was it.

I am humbled to have many memorable and magical moments in my life, and this one will always have a place amongst the magical ones.

Christmas Eve Nightmare

Donna Langille

Every December, a few days before Christmas, Mom trekked to the woods near our house on Big Tancook Island, Nova Scotia, in search of the perfect tree. Armed with a sturdy saw she downed her chosen fir and dragged it across the field to Dad's workshop beside our house. After inspection, Dad bored a few holes here and there along its trunk, inserted additional branches and transformed the tree into a specimen any tree farmer would be proud of.

From there it found a resting place in a designated corner of our living room where it stood bare and forlorn, missing its forest friends—until Christmas Eve when, after supper, Mom and I traditionally trimmed it to perfection.

One particular holiday, two days before Christmas, I arrived home from Halifax where I now lived and worked. Mom listened intently to the radio on Christmas Eve morning when a significant amount of snow was forecast for late in the evening. She suggested we trim the tree during the afternoon but somehow for me that didn't fall into our normal Christmas custom, so we went about the day as usual.

After lunch the snow started, just lightly, but by nightfall a full-blown blizzard howled outside. Dad, on his shift as a crew member aboard the ferry from Tancook to Chester, was away until evening. Following supper Mom and I gathered boxes of ornaments, lights, and trimmings from the storage room in preparation for our evening's work. Before we placed the first ornament on the tree, the power went off, upon which Mom grabbed a flashlight and lit up the area while I decorated.

From her house on Little Tancook, which the ferry also serviced, one of Dad's sisters, Marjorie, through the bands of snow, kept a close eye on the ferry lights in the bay. It tried docking at Little Tancook but poor visibility, high winds and rough seas made every attempt impossible. With great concern for all crew and passengers, including her daughter and family, who were on their way home for the holidays, she kept Mom apprised of the ferry status by phone. The inability to dock on Little Tancook also meant any attempt at Big Tancook would be futile. Aunt Marjorie watched it head back to Chester Harbour, where it took refuge in the lee of close-by islands.

Meanwhile, back in our house, still without power, uncertain about Dad's safe return, our chimney caught fire. Mom quickly threw the contents of a box of baking soda into the kitchen cook stove and as the fire was somewhat quelled, we briskly left the house and took shelter nearby in Dad's workshop. Calmly focused on circumstances of the evening, Mom took it all in stride, kept her head on straight, while I thrived on the excitement. Finally, after what seemed like an eternity, the flames from the chimney became less and less, the roof stayed intact, and we retreated to the house.

Much later that night, when the wind abated, Dad, ferry, all crew and passengers returned home safely. However, snow drifts covered the roads, and Dad, with great difficulty, walked the mile from the wharf to our house. We spent a Christmas Eve like no other, thankful for the positive, happy outcome. Even Santa and all his reindeer found their way through those hazardous flying conditions.

The Moss Girls' Family Christmas

Denise Moss

Christmas made December a busy month in our house. Gifts were bought and parcels were wrapped to be sent by Canada Post to the Giacomini relatives stationed "away" in the Canadian Services. Christmas cards were bought, signed, addressed, and sent to relatives and friends near and far. We four girls prepared a Christmas card for every person in our classroom and the teacher. My mom, Enis, and us girls were baking cookies and making cabbage rolls and sweet-and-sour meatballs to freeze for the crowds of relatives and friends that would visit. Mom also made date squares and mincemeat pie, Dad's favourite, and the magic bar squares and chocolate chip squares, which were the favourites of all the cousins.

We would make a visit a few blocks away, where we would be treated to Pop Shoppe pop from Poppy Giacomini. When there, Mom, Nanny, and Maria would make Christmas pudding in the tin cans and its sauce on the stovetop. The ladies might have also made us bannock from our great-grandmother's Scottish recipe. A fresh snowfall was great to get us in the Christmas spirit. Our family would go to a local farm to have a sleigh ride on the Peters' farm on Mira Road. Aunts, uncles, cousins, and friends would gather and ride while singing sleighing songs such as "Jingle Bells." As the bells on the horses jingled, we rode along the white-covered field and the forest trail. When the sleighs stopped, we fed the horses carrots we had brought.

The Christmas excitement grew as two events unfolded at school. In the night there was a Christmas concert where we all sang carols and the parents and Nanny G came to watch. The last day of school we had a Christmas party with our classmates—cupcakes and cookies—and we distributed Christmas cards with Merry Christmas, Wise Men, and manger scenes on them in individually decorated paper bags taped all along the chalkboard ledge. Later we would each take home our overflowing bag of Christmas cards, and all the Christmas pictures we coloured that month. I would hardly say it was artwork but some went on the fridge at home and some was used to decorate our bedroom doors.

In the evening, when Dad was home from work and the supper dishes were done, we all piled in the station wagon with Dad at the helm, to see the Christmas lights in the city. A stop at Wentworth Park's Bandshell was in order. Mom was sure to get our picture by the nativity scene and also by Santa's reindeer. Then we headed down the Pier to see a whole yard and the neighbourhood street lined with cars, windows down, everyone listening to the Christmas carols. The street was lit like a landing strip. Across from Bernie's Pizza there was always a nativity scene with music playing "Silent Night," toy soldiers, angels, Christmas carolers, and Santa's workshop.

Saturday before Christmas, we were up early to go with all the Moss cousins to cut down our Christmas trees. Mom would make a thermos of hot chocolate and some treats. We would all pile into the station wagon with Aunt Trida and Uncle Tommy. Uncle Ernie and Aunt Deemie would come with the truck. Cousins were all piled in somewhere; there were no seatbelt laws then. Sometimes we would sing all the way.

Mom would pick a tree and we kids would learn to use the bucksaw as we helped Dad saw down the tree. Mom would then say, "That one is too short and bushy for us; we will need that one for Mumma." Then another tree would be too small; that one was for the Moss grandparents. Now the Moss cousins lived in modest-sized homes but the aim was to get the biggest tree that could fit in the room! So we kept searching until all the kids were helping drag our trees out to the truck or on top of the station wagon rooftops. With arms out the windows to assist the tied ropes so the trees did not fall off, we hung onto the trees all the way home. The trees would be placed in a porch or basement of the homes till they thawed and the frost fell out of the boughs. Remember, the bigger the better. One relative was even known to drill holes and stick in extra branches to make it fuller for all the decorations.

Now it was the Sunday before Christmas and we all gathered at one of the relatives' for Christmas Carols. Each year one of the siblings hosted. If it was at Aunt Helen and Uncle Harold's, the cousins Leo and Gordie let us sing into their microphone as they played a few tunes. Uncle Kevin played the guitar for all the Christmas Carols with the few chords he knew, an amazing feat. He had all us kids riled up and participating—singing at the top of our lungs. Aunt Clara and her kids singing with us sure added to our fun. When Aunt Mary and Uncle Allan and Aunt Patsy were home with their families, sometimes there were twenty kids. This certainly became a party, and Uncle Harold and Aunt Deemie joined in the guitar playing. In later years, there were three generations of at least sixteen guitar-playing amateurs singing the Christmas carols.

A few days later, the tree was up; it filled at least a quarter of the room. Dad's large suitcase housed the long, dangly decorations that Mom had purchased or Aunt Maria and Aunt Carolyn had handcrafted for us with love. Soon the large lights were on—

the more the better—and the ornaments were hung from the boughs, filling in any gaps, and the star was at the top. The tinsel and garland surely covered some of the bare spots. The ceiling had garland hung from corner to corner, crossing in the center with an accordion-style, glittery decoration in the centre.

Every doorway had a star or mistletoe at the top, and was adorned along the casings with the many scotch-taped Christmas cards that arrived daily in December from relatives and friends of Mom and Dad from across the country. On the walls, the decorations included Christmas carollers and Santas in the mix. The Christmas Nativity Scene was on a table as well as a ceramic Christmas tree. The crocheted Mr. and Mrs. Claus made by Mom and Dad's godchild, Kim, were on another table. All the girls played with Dad's recorder to make a tape of songs they sang for Mom and Dad—and then they gave it to them as a gift.

At our house on Christmas Eve, the Giacomini grandparents arrived and Nanny G or Mom always gave us new pyjamas. We took a family picture by the tree. Then all the children's eyes bulged and there was so much excitement as the large brown paper parcels with tons of tape that had arrived from Canada Post were brought into the room. Aunt Carolyn and Uncle Wayne and also Aunt Sharon and Uncle Rick sent us four girls each a gift, one for our parents, and one for Nanny and Poppy Giacomini too. Of course Aunt Maria was there. Aunt Maria created homemade gifts for everyone for years. Our homes are filled with decorations and quilts she made with love for us. Maria was like the Fairy Godmother to all her nieces and nephews, and then later to the grandnieces and grandnephews.

The Moss girls were tickled pink as they opened their souvenir dolls from Germany. Mom might have gotten a bell, a souvenir spoon, a cuckoo clock or a wax candle from Schwarzwald, Germany. The record player streamed out Christmas carols. At last, it was a hug and kiss to the adults as the kids went to bed with Dad reading "Twas the night before Christmas."

Then Mom got the turkey on and Dad often had rabbit pie with the neighbours, Judy and Clifford.

Christmas morning came early, as the excited children awoke. The excitement grew as we all ran to the living room to see what Santa had left us under the tree. We all got a new outfit for church, a stocking filled with hard candies and fruit, and wrapped gifts under the tree. After we passed a gift to each other, we tore off the wrapping paper. We found gifts of dolls: Cher, Mrs. Beasley, Christie with the growing hair, and Barbies. There was a small organ, books, and a family game such as *Trivial Pursuit* or *Trouble*. One year I got a book that taught me how to finally solve the rubix cube. I was so excited that I squealed and shook with excitement and Dad got it on the movie camera. I never lived that down!

Mom, the telephone operator and family organizer, always remembered to phone the relatives living away—Great Aunt Edie, Uncle Nicky and Dorothy—to wish them Merry Christmas. We all went to Christmas Mass and then came home to our Christmas turkey dinner with all the trimmings served on Moss Rose china: turkey, gravy, creamy potatoes mashed with butter and milk, carrots, turnips, preserves of beets and pickles, and turkey dressing of bread, potato and poultry seasoning and spices.

We all loved cranberry jelly and sometimes we had cranberries we picked in a bog down near New Victoria. This was topped off with apple pie and ice cream and our favourite blueberry pie and more ice cream. These were blueberries we handpicked in August with Mom, Dad, Nanny G, and Aunt Helen on "The Hill." The big blueberries came from Boisdale where we picked them with the Pennys on the MacSween property. Dinner was prepared by Mom, with us having little things to do to help. My Grandfather Giacomini started a tradition of orange pop as the treat at Christmas. Oh, what a poultice! Then we danced to "The Merry Christmas Polka" with Dad.

In the afternoon we were off in the car to visit both grandparents and see all the cousins. Christmas Day and Boxing Day we visited and had something to eat and drink at every aunt and uncle's house. We were sure to have a porkpie at Trida's and lemon meringue pie and ham with mustard at Nanny Moss's.

The days started early and ended late and somehow they all visited us too. I think we drove in caravans to each place so we would all be together for days! Other days that week, Mom made Cream Chicken, a recipe from Aunt Helen Mozvick's Hungarian husband, Mom's famous Italian lasagna, and her spaghetti and meatballs. Then in the days that followed we visited Great Aunts Dot and Ette, and we liked to play with little toys found in tea packages, and we played the piano with great Aunt Beulah at our great-grandfather Woodburn's house. Mom also had some great aunts come eat with us: Great Aunt Kay and Great Aunt Helen. We visited many friends and relatives like the Pennys, the Martins, and the Lundrigans, where we were sure to have some of Patsy's famous shortbreads. There were chocolates and candies overflowing their dishes all week at all the homes.

At each house we played new games with the children. If it snowed we all met at a hill and went tobogganing, the more on the sled the better. Dad and some of the others cleared the snow off The Pond for all the Moss cousins to skate. This pond on East Broadway hill was behind the Moss grandparents' home. We would go in and warm our hands and dry our mittens by the potbelly wood stove where we each had had our first cups of tea with canned milk along with a milk lunch cookie.

On New Year's Eve the parents all went to the New Year's Eve Ball at St. Theresa Hall or the Holy Redeemer Gym. We kids had treats: maybe Bernie's pizza, Napoli pizza, pop and chips. Sometimes we had a different family "from away" in each bedroom of our home. The kids had a big slumber party. There was laughter, excitement, running up and down the basement stairs to get food and bring more cousins down to play, and all the kids were so happy. My Mom was called "Johnny Abbass" because she took pictures of everything. Dad kept the record player going all Christmas with Jim Reeves and Perry Como, and children's favourites.

Another great Moss family Christmas! What a great Christmas for four little Moss girls!

Dedicated with love to my parents Enis and Gordie

I Got a Job!

Winston Ruck

I started at the steel plant in 1940. That's quite a story. December 27, 1940, I considered as the happiest day of my life.

December the 27th is when I got a job at the steel plant. I will never forget that day as long as I live. Because at that time we had been living with my aunt. We had been living with my aunt from the time my father had passed on in 1936. And that was the height of the Depression. Very difficult. Not only for ourselves, but for everybody. Including the white community as well. Those were difficult times.

As I indicated, we five boys—five brothers—we were living with my aunt (Mrs. Viola Calender) following the death of my father. Her husband was working on a part-time basis. You can imagine the load that they suddenly found themselves with, with the advent of five boys—hungry boys with appetites!

But we were resourceful because we were taught that way, from the time we were small, to look after yourself. And we used to help the best as we could, by going up to the old Marsh Dump and bringing home coal during the summer months. Because it was hard for them to find the money to buy a ton of coal. It didn't cost $5—a half a ton cost $2.50 in those days. That was hard to come up with, that $2.50. Now, we weren't the only ones that did it. All the other boys in the community did the same thing. That was their way of assisting their families. Go up to the Marsh Dump.

You'd pick the coal from the dump. We carried it on our backs. We weren't very big or we weren't very strong. But we managed to bring coal down to keep the house going all winter without them having to purchase coal.

And the same with the wood supply, we looked after that. And they had a few chickens and a few ducks there. That was our job, to feed them. They would kill them off, particularly around Christmas time or Easter time. And things of that nature.

And that was our way of making a contribution to the house. And Mr. Calender, my aunt's husband, he appreciated that very, very much. He used to always tell us. As a matter of fact, he even built an additional shed so we could put more coal in.

And so, I was getting older. I used to get an odd job here and there. I used to go around assisting people in building homes, basements. Take the wheelbarrow and help pour the concrete. The city was putting through a sewer and a waterline on Maloney Street, back in the late '30s. And I got a job on that. On digging. Pick and shovel. Hard, hard work. I was only about fifteen, sixteen at the time.

And that was a tough digging, because there was a lot of rock going up the hill. All rock. They had to dynamite continually to break through the rock.

So those were the things that we did at that time. I was going to the Academy, in Grade 10, Grade 11. Then during the summer months, that's what we would do.

I also worked on the beer truck. My father was a very prominent man and managed to secure the contract for hauling the beer to the Pier. Billy Hill—another prominent Liberal at that time—had the contract for the town liquor store. There were only two at that time. So after (my father) died, his partner carried on with that. And occasionally I'd get a job in a truck, hauling beer. And then, when he had no hauling, I'd get a job with Billy Hill.

So while we were working hauling the beer, we'd go down to the General Office at the Steel Plant. Because the General Office started to hire people then in late '39 and '40, because of the war. And we put our name in during the summer—all of us did at that time . . . .

And in order for you to get a job, you had to be there when they called your name. You used to sit around out there for a couple of hours. But you couldn't do that every day because some days you probably got another job and you've gone someplace else, or you've gone to play ball. And that would be the day they came out and they called off your name. If you weren't there, they forgot about you. They hired anyone whose name they called up was there. That's the way that worked.

So this day in question, I had my name in for quite some time, all that summer. They were hiring people sporadically, here and there. December 27, 1940, I was working for Billy Hill. And a call came down to the dispatcher, the agent for CN—he checked all the beer that was taken off the cars. Man by the name of Bricky Williams. My aunt had called him and told him that they wanted me at the General Office. Get up to the General Office. I assumed that they were going to hire me.

I jumped off the car, grabbed my hat and coat jacket. And I ran all the way to the General Office because, like I said, if you didn't get there that day, forget it. And I never had that much time. And I got there. Got into the door of the hiring officer. And I was the only one there—it was pretty near quitting time. And I got in, I was huffing and puffing. I remember Cecil MacPherson saying to me, "Son, you're all in." I said, "Yes." I said, "I ran all the way in here." "Well," he said, "sit down, sit down." I was all in. Said, "Sit down, sit down, sit down." He gave me a chair to sit down. And he went in and got my card and number. He said, "Don't worry," he said, "we're going to hire you."

I'm telling you, those were the greatest words I ever heard in my life. (*Why?*) To get a job! (*Well, you had a job.*) Oh, yeah, but this job we had was only sporadic.

You may get two days this week. That was the most you could get. (*And how good a job were you going to get at the steel plant?*) A steady job working seven days a week. You were going to get a steady job, in the steel plant. So you were sure of a pay every week. And you're getting the wages that they paid at that time, which was $3.63 a day, I think it was. It was 43 1/2 cents an hour—do the arithmetic on that. ($3.48 a day.) Seven days a week. Seven days a week. You had to work seven days to get you a $20 bill. You had to work seven days a week to see a $20 bill. 'Cause they had to take off for benefits at that time, and some other deductions that they made.

So in order for you to see a $20 bill—my eyes were like that! Twenty dollars to me! In my pay bag. When I got my first seven days and saw $20 in a pay envelope that belonged to me! Merciful heaven, that was—talk about being on Cloud Nine.

But, I got ahead in my story. So, he hired me that day. He said, "I'm not even going to bother to send you for an examination. It's too late. But you come back Monday morning and we'll send you in to see Dr. Lynch"—was the company doctor at that time. And they had a little clinic hospital right there, next to the General Office. But he gave me my clock card, and best of all, he gave me my check number—1057. That was my number. Look, I was so grateful. "I thank you, I thank you, I thank you. Very very much." Now I've got a check number in my hand.

And when he gave me that, that—opened the door for me. By this time everybody was pretty well gone now. It was getting on to 5 o'clock, and they generally closed around 4:30, so I was pretty close—I just got in under the wire.

I took that and I ran all the way home. You heard that song,

"I ran all the way home." I came bursting in the door, and I said, "Aunt Vee, Aunt Vee, I got hired! Here's my check number. I've got to go to work tonight, on the backshift." This was 11 to 7 then.

And she was so grateful. She hugged me, and she cried. "Okay," she put on her coat. She went up to the store—one of the merchants, Jewish merchants, in the Pier. Whatever money she made, she bought me overalls and boots, work gloves, and socks, and a lunch can.

And I went to work that night on the backshift. I was seventeen years old, seventeen and a half. Talk about gladness and happiness—that was it. And of course, everybody, all my other brothers and two cousins, were all happy because I got the job, because now I could visualize that I would be able to ease the finances of the household. Well, five boys!

Winston Ruck became the first Black president of the Steelworkers Union.

Our Christmas Tree

Teresa McNutt

Christmastime is an important time of year for my partner. While we were getting to know one another, he proudly told me he grew up in the Christmas Tree Capital of the World! He is from the South Shore, and his father grew Christmas trees. His cousins still grow trees in New Ross and export them all over the world. There is indeed a sign on the highway announcing New Ross as the Christmas tree hotspot. My boyfriend grew up in Canaan, near Chester, and still owns the land from which his father harvested Christmas trees.

My sweetheart had a difficult life, as many of us did growing up in relative poverty in rural Nova Scotia in the 1960s and 1970s. He was often unwell as a child, and was not always able to be out playing in the woods with his friends as much as he would have liked. He fondly remembers the days he rode his dirt bike with other boys in his neighbourhood as some of his happiest times. He was told as a child that he would not be a good fit for a manual labour job, so he'd better do well in school.

As his school friends and relatives worked jobs in the community, in the woods of Lunenburg County, or lobster fishing, my partner worked hard in university. He studied chemistry and math at Saint Mary's University, and loved his time there. He did well, and won a gold medal for having the highest marks upon graduating! He was accepted into medical school at Dalhousie University and he became a surgeon. When the new Regional Hospital was opening in Sydney, he came to Cape Breton to work and settle down.

For the first few years, he continued to go home in autumn to assist his father in cutting and selling Christmas trees and making wreaths.

Several years later, after an illness, he moved into a condominium. Daily life became enough of a chore, and little extras and comforts were sometimes missed. He bought himself a condominium tree. It was a little faux tabletop tree with one red ball, and he had a few decorations that patients had given him. It was hard times, but he made the most of it. He often phoned his cousins to hear about the tree harvest and business, and missed having a real Christmas tree.

Our first Christmas together, I pulled a real Christmas tree up the stairs to the tiny attic apartment I was renting on George Street. I was amazed that he could look at the tree and say how old it was and how much it had been pruned. He asked about the tree's provenance at the lot, and was thrilled to know it came from New Ross and he knew the growers!

That was a very happy Christmas for both of us in that little apartment. When I bought a tiny house near the Regional Hospital, he helped me pick out a proper tree stand that could hold a big tree. We had trees that touched the ceiling of that little house, and when they were lit, you could see them from the hospital driveway.

When we decided to build a house and live together, it was understood we would never have a fake Christmas tree. When we looked at the plans of our future home, we talked about where we would put the Christmas tree.

As the early December moving day approached, I developed a stomach ailment that sapped my energy at a time I was packing and organizing the move. By moving day all I was able to eat were three bites of chicken. Disappointed, I realized that unpacking enough to get a Christmas tree decorated was not going to happen. So we put the condominium tree on one of the cardboard boxes and made the most of it. It was fun mixing old and new, starting new traditions. We put a sparkly snowman decoration outside, and planned to add to him every year until we looked like the Griswolds! We were just happy to be in our new and final home, and excited for the future.

The first year in our new home was a whirlwind of changes and continuing to settle in. In anticipation for our first Exciting All Decorated Real Christmas Together, I got fluffy flannel sheets with Christmas trees on them. I got Christmas placemats and tablecloths. I got Christmas guest towels. I put up all of our decorations, as well as the vintage ones that had come from his parents' home. The big day to get the tree was coming, and I wanted it to be perfect.

We were hearing there wasn't much on the lots. His cousins were saying they were selling out quickly. When I went into the lot, the owner got a panicked look on his face. He knew us and knows my partner's background. He said, "We were really busy last week!" There were only about half a dozen trees left and they looked kind of sad. Some had broken branches, and some had what my Sweetheart explained were holes from either frost or deer, that the grower attempted to prune and thicken over the next year. At home, my partner told me that, normally, to sell a tree like ours you'd have to hold the tree and rotate your body, so only the best side is showing to the customer but it gives the appearance of showing the whole tree!

We had a wonderful day decorating that wonky crooked tree and drinking hot chocolate. We rotated the tree and straightened it in the stand. Then we rotated it again.

We found an inchworm making its way along a branch. We googled to see if it was some type of invasive pest and since it wasn't, it continued to live its life on the tree. Finally, my partner said that his father would have left a tree like that in the woods.

Throughout the holiday, as we watered and lit that funny tree, I saw him smile the way he does when he is nostalgic about his years spending time in the woods of Lunenburg County with his friends and cousins. We put the condominium tree on a side table. It didn't matter how crooked the real tree was or how many branches were broken. It was our first Christmas tree in our house, and it made us happy and hopeful for a bright future with many more Christmas trees to come.

The Courageous Captain
of the *Cleo*

Francis W. Grant

Other writers have told the story of the brigantine *Cleo*. They have recounted it accurately, and nothing can be

added or subtracted to make it more meaningful or more interesting. But whereas my grandfather, Captain Francis Grant, was
master of that stout little ship for several of his earlier years at
sea, leaving her in 1864 to take command of the barque *Gipsy*, I
would like to tell the tale as he told it, as closely as my memory
will recall it from my mid-teens, plus the assistance of pencilled
notes made by his eldest son, my Uncle John Grant, which I have
before me.

Grandfather had no unusual adventures in the *Cleo*. His
period of time aboard her was quite routine and uneventful. But
for young Captain Borden Marsh, who followed him in the brigantine, a terrible ordeal lay ahead which would have taken the
vessel to the bottom had it not been for the versatility, determination and courage of the youthful skipper from Economy,
Nova Scotia. And for that courageous young master mariner,
Grandfather had the highest praise, knowing from experience
what it all meant.

The story of the *Cleo's* ordeal begins at Glace Bay, Cape
Breton, where she had taken on a full cargo of coal for Boston.
Sailing craft, dependent on the wind, knew no holidays, and with
a fair wind blowing, Captain Marsh made sail and got under
way Christmas Day, 1868. It was a fine and pleasant day, with
no indication of heavy weather coming, and all seemed to bode
well for the voyage.

As darkness came on that evening, following the fine weather
of the day, the wind suddenly shifted and at once developed into
a roaring gale. The fore-topgallant mast carried away and caused
considerable difficulty in the clearing away of the tangle of such
a mishap. Then as the night wore on, the wind shifted again, and
to the opposite quarter of the compass. It increased from a gale
to a veritable hurricane, and with it came driving, blinding snow.
For seven days the screaming gale never eased for a moment, and
the shifting wind had built up cross-seas—seas which can wrack
a wooden ship to ruin in short order.

The Courageous Captain of the *Cleo*

The *Cleo* laboured greatly in the cross-seas, and huge seas swept over her, carrying everything before them with their terrific power. The boats were plucked from their fastenings like match-sticks and disappeared in the maelstrom, together with everything else on the deck. Even the bulwarks began to go.

All the while the ship was taking in water, and to keep afloat the seamen were compelled to man the two pumps continually. It was pump or drown, and the men toiled with the strength of desperation in spite of aching muscles and lack of rest. They could do no more than hold their own, and to add to their predicament the pumps began to fail. The leathers on the plungers had become so worn they would no longer raise the water. Captain Marsh removed the plungers and replaced the leathers but still the pumps refused to draw properly. Without the pumps the *Cleo* would soon sink, she was filling so rapidly.

It should be explained that pumps on the smaller wooden ships of sail were very simple contrivances. A pump was merely a good straight log of the required length, bored through from end to end the size of the plunger desired. The plunger was connected to the handle by a rod of iron.

Captain Marsh concluded correctly that so much wear from continual pumping had enlarged the inside of the wooden pump in the area where the plunger moved up and down. He took the rod and plunger out again, cut several inches off the rod and bent the end in the galley fire to form a new hook to attach to the pump handle. The repairs put the pumps back in working order, and the resourceful captain and his crew of five breathed easier again. It was still a struggle of constant pumping, but there was renewed encouragement that they might survive.

Driving before the wind, the *Cleo* had run far to the south and there was no hope whatever of beating back to their destination. The only course open was to head for the West Indies. But now another problem confronted Captain Marsh. He was running short of food as he had put aboard very little more than what he expected would be used on the run to Boston. He had no choice but to dole out sparingly such as remained. However, his crew understood the situation very well and willingly accepted the rationing.

Still another and extremely serious problem presented itself to the young skipper. With the bulwarks ripped away by the huge seas, the deck had no protection whatever. Every wave poured over the *Cleo* and down around the stanchions that had supported the bulwarks. The oakum was thus being lost from the seams, and they must be recaulked or the end would come in a few hours.

Captain Marsh would not order one of his crew to do the terribly dangerous and difficult job, but elected to undertake it himself. He was lowered overboard in a rope sling and down the side of the rolling, pitching brigantine. With a mallet in one hand and a caulking iron in the other, he began the arduous task of driving oakum into the openings from which it had gone. To do so he had to strike a few blows when the ship rolled away from him. Then, when she rolled back he was under water until the vessel rolled up once more. He would hammer in a little more oakum while above water, get a few good breaths of air, and go under again. This went on and on until half drowned and utterly exhausted he could do no more, though more was really still needed. But courageous Borden Marsh was beyond continuing. When they hauled him on board he was in a state of near collapse, and no wonder. He hadn't had more than snatches of sleep or a fraction of a meal for several days. Though he had been unable to complete the job, he had done enough to greatly slow the leaks, and the weather was showing signs of improving.

Yes, the weather was improving, and the *Cleo* had reached warm waters, but there was now not one bite of food left on board. Nor did they sight another ship, and for two more weeks nobody on the battered brigantine had a thing to eat. Fortunately they still had a good supply of drinking water, and could at least quench their thirst.

When Captain Borden Marsh sailed the *Cleo* into the harbour of Saint Thomas, forty days had passed since leaving Glace Bay. They were starving, and the first thing the captain did was to make a signal for food to be brought out to the vessel. He had saved the *Cleo*, the lives of the crew of five as well as his own life, and the cargo of coal was saved too. What a man! No wonder Grandfather and all the other sea captains who knew Bordon Marsh admired him with utmost sincerity.

An Acadian Fisherman Recalls Christmas as a Child ✦ ✦ ✦

Rosie Aucoin Grace

Being raised in a household with elders, I often listened to stories about a time when our ancestors struggled to survive, a life of simplicity but yet for many they derived so much joy with so little. The parents often barely had the means but they worked hard and made wonderful sacrifices and efforts to make Christmas special for their loved ones. The children's expectations were very minimal and they were content with anything that was left in their stockings. No matter what they received, they were happy and believed in the magic of Christmas.

I remember years ago interviewing a very well-known and prosperous fisherman from Petit-Étang, the late Wilfred (à Jenny) Chiasson. Of course the discussion was mostly fixated on his life on the sea but we spoke about his growing up in the village of Chéticamp and some of his tales intrigued me. When he described Christmas, I remember how he smiled and softly expressed, "When I was a child, Christmas certainly was not like today, not at all! In those days, you were lucky if you received some des mix (hard candy). Sometimes, you got the odd item but not much.

"Christmas was not festive like present day," said Chiasson. He added, "I do not recall that our family ever put up a Christmas tree or decorations. At the time, in Petit-Étang, we had no electricity. We only got this luxury around the year 1947, approximately ten years later than other areas. I guess without electricity to add some lights, we did not bother putting up a tree."

Chiasson continued, "Some families did decorate a tree. They did not run for decorations dans les shoppes downtown. They would use old Christmas cards saved year after year and bells to fill up the tree. Christmas might not have been fancy like today, but it was still very exciting. We recognized and appreciated that this was a special time of the year. We always hoped that we would receive something, anything."

He added, "During my childhood years, of course I believed in Santa Claus. It was exciting and fun!

"It was a time when my mother would make meat pies and more fancy baking," said Chiasson. "To our delight, she used to make tamarin (hard taffy) and it was delicious. Also something we so looked forward to, a visit to the store to see the big jars filled with candies, peppermint and chocolates. Bah c'était beau et si bon! (Oh it was so beautiful to see and so good). They used to have the loose chocolates back then, instead of boxes, huge jars of them. You would buy them individually and this was quite the treat! Ah yes, those were special times . . . . That was just the way life was then."

As Wilfred spoke about these Christmases, it became clear to me that these cherished memories were embedded in his heart, never to be forgotten.

For most of us, the origins of our Christmas traditions are

long lost. We do not necessarily remember their origins, if we ever knew. We perform the same rituals as our parents because they are nostalgic; they make us feel warm and fuzzy, like we are carrying on something important that links us to our families and the happy times growing up.

There are so many ways to celebrate the holiday season that do not involve gift giving. Like putting up Christmas tree decorations, baking Christmas cookies, watching Christmas movies, caroling, attending tree lightings, taking in some Christmas concerts, listening to festive music, perhaps being a member of the local choir or helping to decorate the Church, sledding, skating outdoors, attending Christmas markets, crafting, a family drive to see the Christmas decorations, participating in a local toy drive or other fundraisers—and the list goes on.

No matter what you choose to do with your family and friends, celebrating old traditions, or making new ones, is what makes this season the most magical and wonderful time of the year!

Santa's Shoes

Ronald Labelle

When did we all stop believing in Santa Claus? If, like one of my good friends, you were a young child whose siblings included a know-it-all older sister, you probably remember the day when she declared to you, in no uncertain terms, that Santa Claus was just a make-believe character invented by parents. But for many of us, our loss of faith in the true Santa Claus happened gradually. As we developed through childhood, doubts appeared in our minds, and eventually we came to the sad conclusion that

Christmas gifts didn't come from the North Pole. Our suspicions about the veracity of Santa's existence came from the little clues we picked up here and there. But what stands out for me is the Christmas when my cousin Guy discovered one of those clues that made him wonder whether Santa Claus was real.

On each Christmas day, our family would gather at my grandparents' house, along with our cousins, their parents and a few great aunts and uncles. For the adults, the highlight of the day was no doubt the big Christmas dinner my grandmother prepared with her helpers. But for us children, the most important part of the celebration was certainly the arrival of Santa Claus himself, who brought a gift for each of us.

At some point in the afternoon, someone would call out, seeing Santa approaching the house, and my grandfather would go to the front door, where he would ceremoniously let him in.

In all the years I spent growing up next door to my grandparents' house, I never saw anyone but Santa arrive by the main entrance. Everyone always entered by the side door that led directly into the kitchen, even the priest. Only Santa Claus walked up the front steps and was ushered into the hallway in the centre of the house.

On that fateful occasion, we all ran excitedly to the living room when we heard Santa Claus had arrived. The jolly fellow entered with a loud "Ho! Ho! Ho!" and sat down in my grandfather's big armchair, ready to take each of us on his knee. When it was my cousin's turn, he approached Santa but then hesitated. Looking down, he said, "Le Père Noël a les souliers de Papa!" It seems that, rather than wearing his usual black winter boots, Santa Claus had on the exact same type of shoes that my uncle usually wore. It also happened that my Uncle Maurice was absent at that very moment. My cousin was a smart kid—he eventually became a health care professional—and he must have found it very odd that Santa Claus would be wearing shoes identical to those of his temporarily absent father.

Being a year younger than my cousin, the incident didn't trouble me. I only understood what had happened later on, as the story was retold during subsequent Christmas celebrations. My grandmother was always fond of telling the tale, and I think that explains why it has become such an enduring memory for me.

Santa Claus continued to make his yearly visits for a few more Christmases, until all the children were past the age when they believed in him, and I'm sure that in subsequent years, whoever was playing the role made sure they had on the complete costume, boots and all. Little children are very observant, and they are especially aware of everything that happens at ground level, because their point of view is much closer to the ground than that of grownups. The shoes, it seems, were a giveaway. I would continue to believe in Santa for another year or two, but I am sure my cousin Guy was no longer convinced of Santa Claus's existence after the Christmas when he saw him wearing his father's shoes.

Professor Cobbywobble's Most Delicious Christmas

Clare Currie

Travel away for Christmas? No, but thank you very much! It wouldn't be Christmas if Professor Cobbywobble left his home, somewhere North of Cameria. It was a small place very far away, but it was his home. It is almost impossible to find it on a map, unless you really know where to look.

Christmas never disappointed Cobbywobble too much, or excited him for that matter. Every day of every year, Cook rang his bell at exactly six minutes and six seconds after six o'clock in the morning. Nothing ever changed much for Professor Cobbywobble, so Christmas was no different. He ate his Yuletide breakfast, which was the same breakfast he had every day—a crumpet with butter and a hot cup of tea. Very hot. And pour the milk in first, please. That was how Cobbywobble always had it. Then, he would water his houseplants, make his bed and start his work day. He did very important work. Nobody knew what it was exactly, but it was important.

Everywhere Professor Cobbywobble went, his little dog Bonnie went with him. After his breakfast, he would put his saucer on the floor, and Bonnie would have some of his tea in that. Bonnie was a gentle and happy dog, and she and the professor were always together.

After breakfast, Christmas was the same as every day too, except that he gave Cook a new book of maps, and that was that. This year, Cook was invited home to Cape Breton for Christmas. "Never heard of it," Cobbywobble said loudly to poor, tired Cook. Cook lowered his head and whispered, "And if you ever came, you'd never want to leave, Professor." Cobbywobble looked around at his tiny room in his tiny house and thought maybe it would be nice to travel a little, to see another part of the world than North of Cameria. As he left Cook for the night and began to read under his lamp, he thought, That's it. I am going to Cape Breton with Cook for Christmas! It hadn't crossed Cook's mind that he would be taking his boss home with him, but there it was planned anyway.

Hmmm . . . what if the bed isn't comfortable?

Would his houseplants be okay?

They might not have crumpets there.

"What should I pack, Cook? What do I need to know about this place?"

"Nothing, really," Cook answered, "Just nice people, sir. And pack your long underwear."

The trip from North of Cameria took two days in his old car, and both travellers were tired but happy to be in Cape Breton. What an interesting place this is, thought Cobbywobble. They passed a painted Scotsman on the side of a mountain, a teepee reaching up to the sky, and the smell of salt water and fresh air was so welcoming! It looked like a million Christmas trees were along the side of the road, with a soft dusting of fresh snow on every one. Christmas was in two days, and they could feel excitement in the air!

Cook was up with the crows the next morning, and had a very long list of items to pick up today. He was to travel to New Waterford, Whitney Pier, Sydney Mines, and Mabou Coal Mines. Cobbywobble insisted on going with him, expecting a normal grocery trip.

As they drove into New Waterford, they came upon Horyl's Meat Shop. Cook went in, and returned with the longest coil of processed meat he had ever seen. "Kielbasa," said Cook. "It is a favourite for Christmas Eve." Cobbywobble could never imagine anyone being able to eat all of that stinky stuff in a year, let alone a holiday!

Then off to Mrs. Wozniak's house in Whitney Pier, to purchase three dozen of her famous pirogies. He made Cobbywobble promise not to touch the food on the way home. But it would be difficult. The smell of those fried balls of potato and cheese, as they hit each pothole, was almost too much! He was getting hungrier by the minute.

"Oops—I almost forgot about Joseph Morgan, the Newfoundlander with the house by the water." Two pots of baked beans and some figgy duff. Oh, the crates were smelling in the old car more than ever, and everything smelled absolutely delicious!!

Maybe Cook was onto something here, thought Professor

Cobbywobble. Maybe Cape Breton is a good place to spend Christmas!

Next stop: Sydney Mines, to Mrs. Bandini's house. She had a huge container of spaghetti and meatballs ready for them. They were the biggest meatballs Cobbywobble had ever seen!

Last stop? Mabou Coal Mines. Now that was a long drive! Poor Cobbywobble was weak with hunger by the time he got there, and Mr. MacGregor invited them right in. He said, "Have some tea and an oatcake before you head back.

"Oatcake? You like the oatcakes? Wait until you try the fish cakes!"

"Cakes made out of oats is one thing. But cakes made out of fish? That's just too much," said Cobbywobble. "Or figgy duff, or kielbasa for that matter? What is going on in this place? I have never even heard tell of most of these things, and they don't sound very delicious to me!"

That was the last thing he said for a while. As Mr. MacGregor poured him his tea, he added the milk first. Then he topped it with hot, delicious tea. He demonstrated to Cobbywobble how to properly dunk the corner of the oatcake into the tea cup and let it drip off for a few seconds on the saucer. It may have been the best thing Cobbywobble ever ate! Boy oh boy, he should have come to Cape Breton years ago for Christmas; it was so full of kind, lovely people and the most delicious foods ever!

As they headed back home that night, Cook remembered one more very important stop. The Alasfars always had fatyers set aside for him, as he would order them every Christmas for his family. It wouldn't be a holiday without these delicious pastries! Cobbywobble shook his head in amazement. The scent of mint wafted through their home, and it was heavenly.

As he helped Cook carry all of the food to the kitchen, he asked, "What is your proper name, Cook?"

"Harry, Sir. And this is my sister Nora. We spend every Christmas here in Cape Breton, surrounded by the sea, salt water and all of the wonderful people living here. And of course, all of their delicious foods! I cook for you all year, Sir, so when we come home, Nora and I order food from our friends across the island, and don't cook all week! We have the best of every kind of food you'll ever find, right here."

Nora nodded in agreement, her arms folded across her chest. "We are lucky to have the nicest, kindest and best neighbours ever." Cobbywobble shook his head in wonder. "I should have come to Cape Breton many Christmases ago, Cook . . . . Er, I mean Harry." Harry and Nora chimed in agreement, "And then you should come every Christmas in the future!"

Cobbywobble smiled from ear to ear, thinking how lucky he was to have such lovely friends, and wonderful food!

It truly was the most delicious Christmas ever.

Christmas Wine
A Family Memory of Jim Kelly

Joanne Kelly

I was taking out a bottle of wine and thinking that maybe I should buy a case of wine to give out as Christmas gifts when a real story about your father made me laugh out loud.

Last Christmas I had this same thought and went out and bought a number of bottles of wine. It was a rainy cold day, just like today. I managed with some difficulty, because of my immobility, to get to the liquor store and purchase the wine, and get home. The rain was awful.

I managed to drive home and text the caregiver that I needed help bringing the loot in. She was busy at the moment so I entered the house without the bags and just left instructions to bring the wine in when it would be convenient for the caregiver.

I then headed up to my room to write a few cards to go with the wine, and to prepare some other gifts.

I was deeply engrossed in the card writing and was not paying attention to what was going on downstairs. The caregiver was equally engrossed in her activity of preparing supper downstairs in the kitchen.

About half an hour passed when the caregiver and I wondered what Jim was up to.

The cards having been written, and supper now ready, it was time to check on Jim.

The caregiver had dutifully brought in the wine. It was on display on the dining room table. And there we found Jim proudly opening all the wine for the tasting. He was sure that he was doing a good job and hoping to have company for dinner to help us decide which wine was the best.

Jim loved having company. He enjoyed inspecting his choice of wine and encouraged comments on it. Foxy devil, Jim had lots of wine last Christmas! And the caregiver didn't even drink!

Take My Turkey . . . Please!

Donna D'Amour

Could I offer you a **hot turkey sandwich**, a bowl of home-made turkey soup, chunk of turkey pot pie? Have mercy on the overstocked. I'm a simple person. I don't ask for much. I specifically didn't ask for much turkey this Christmas.

"Just get a small one, Honey," I said. "There are only four of us, two of us are very tiny and one of us has a teeny appetite for leftovers."

"Where's your spirit," he grinned. "It's Christmas. You never know who'll drop in."

He bought a 25-pounder.

The fictional Whos, who supposedly crave leftover turkey, didn't show. We had Whos who dropped in for a peek at the tree; Whos who dropped in to extend season's greetings; Whos who dropped in for one small drink, but they were all pre-stuffed.

"Couldn't fit one more bit," they swore.

"Just came from Mother's, had to loosen my belt two notches."

"Can't even look at food."

Tell me about it. I've taken that bird from roast pan to table, refrigerator to casserole, pie plate to soup pot, even from fry pan to microwave, and I'll swear it's gained weight. Not surprising. It happens to everyone else this time of year.

I've done Canadian, English, American, Italian, Chinese and Indian but I haven't seen the last of it. I dream that one morning I will open my fridge and see space. I long to sit down to a meal of fish or beef. I don't mean to be wasteful. I know there are thousands starving in the world. I know it's good wholesome food. But no matter how I disguise it, my stomach rebels . . . not turkey again!

Every year it's the same. Hubby gets visions of Christmas tables only a Walton would recognize. Uncles, aunts, grandparents, cousins, neighbours, all around a table which stretches forever.

The problem is . . . that's not our table. Our relatives are few and far away. Our neighbours and friends have their own tables. It's four of us against the bird—but he forgets.

I guess I can't knock the man for being generous. Besides it'll all be over by New Year's Day. He's already begun preparation for that. He's been huddled with a magazine all morning and he's got me curious. Something about the look in his eye as he left the house has me wondering.

I pick up the magazine and it falls open to a colourful page. "Olden Days Feast," the caption reads. There in the centre of a ten-foot table sits a whole roast pig with a rosy apple stuffed in its mouth.

Really have to run. I've got to make it to the butcher shop fast. If there's one thing I don't wish for in the New Year, it's 365 days of leftover pork.

Orphaned for Christmas

Fay Wambolt

My usual stories are happy or funny, but I find myself thinking more and more about when our parents are no longer here to celebrate with us. My father passed away in 2000, and if you knew my father you would understand just how much Christmas meant to us in our family. We always had Christmas Eve dinner at my grandparents' house; then we would head home for what I as a child believed was the real fun part of Christmas Eve. We would first rush to get into our pyjamas and claim our spot on the floor next to the tree—then out came the making of the perfect Christmas Eve snack. This snack consisted of a glass of Pepsi and a bowl of chips. We made sure to each have our own small bowl; we never wanted someone else's hand in our bowl. And the saving the best for last was the choosing of chocolate. Once all this was settled we would be ready to watch "A Christmas Carol." After that it was off to bed.

As we grew older and had families of our own, we still kept our traditions and added more. Christmas Day was so chaotic.

Not only were we trying to round up the families but also trying to help Mom with the turkey, entertain the kids and stop my father from picking on the kids to the point were they were crying. Have you ever been in a room with sixteen kids getting gifts from three different families? It's like putting a chocolate cake on a table and telling them not to touch it. It never works. So here we were all trying to open gifts, remember who they were from and trying to be appreciative all at the same time. Talk about multitasking at its best.

This was us at our best and sometimes our worst, but always with full stomachs, happy hearts and lots of love. I remember when my dad passed away. My first Christmas without him was so frightening, I kept thinking how was I going to react around my family, especially Mom. My heart was breaking, but I knew I had to put on a brave face and continue our traditions.

It's funny how Christmas can make us both happy and sad at the same time. To this day I start feeling a bit of dread and anxiety leading up to Christmas. I even at times feel guilt creep in. How can I enjoy such a day when this day meant so much to my dad?

Fast forward to 2015, my father-in-law passed away and now my wife was experiencing the same feelings I have had for so many years. We talked often about this and how important it was to always make sure our moms were okay and feeling all the love our families had to give.

You see, my mom always tells me she doesn't like Christmas. One day I asked her why she no longer likes Christmas and reminded her that there was a time when she loved the holiday. She said it's never been the same since Da was gone, and she said even though we have a family of twenty-plus on this day that holds so much joy and excitement for many people, she actually feels alone.

That one statement broke my heart. How can we as children help our parents to feel included, wanted and loved? I have spent so many years making sure my mom felt this in her heart. I think although she feels loneliness at Christmas it's not so much the day; it is the fact that everyone around her has a significant other or parents or siblings.

What Mom doesn't realize is that she is what makes us feel loved. When my wife's father passed, she started the same journey of making sure her mom felt included, even though her mom wasn't a full Christmas-celebration type. My wife, like me, would make sure all the immediate family would gather for a Christmas dinner and the usual chaos of gift-giving. This year was hard, as my wife's mom passed away. My heart was broken for her and her family.

Christmas came and it was very different. Everyone was making efforts to create the usual Christmas dinner but it was not the usual dinner. There was no gathering of the whole family. There were a few at one house and others decided to go it alone. Wherever they ended up that day they all felt the same loneliness.

We talked about what her family core would look like now that both parents are no longer with us, and one night as we were talking over a cup of tea my wife looked at me and said, "I'm now an orphan." Her statement hit me like a ton of bricks. I started thinking about my own mom and how I would feel if something were to happen, would I feel the same? Are we really orphans once our parents are gone? I know those of us that have our own families may not feel this to the same degree but for some, even though we have our own children, sometimes it is not the same as being the child.

To be honest I am still processing Cathy's statement and cannot answer that for myself. I still have my mom and I plan to make every moment count. As for my wife, she no longer has her parents but she is loved deeply. Until my last breath I will make sure our Christmases will be filled with love, laughter and joy. We may all feel sad or lonely at Christmas, but it's a season where we also feel happy and loved. So my question to each of you is, are we really orphans or can the love of family and friends make the season a little brighter with each passing year?

So this year look around you and if you have that sad or lonely feeling in your heart, reach out and take the hand closest to you, give it a squeeze—and I bet you it will squeeze back with love.

"There was always food and fiddling"

Archie Neil Chisholm

When I was a boy, my family had very little in the way of worldly goods. My father was a teacher and teacher's pay was small in those days. At Christmas, it was a struggle to provide even a little bit extra for the nine children in our family. But our expectations were different then, and we were delighted to get an exotic treat like an orange and a few candies in our woollen socks. We all knew early who Santa really was, but we didn't let on; we played the game to make it more fun for our parents.

There was often a big box that arrived at our house before Christmas, from relatives in the Boston States or other places. It was full of used clothing, something for everybody, and we looked forward to that. When some of the older children moved away on their own, they sent a little cash so that there was something for the younger children at home at Christmas. We seemed to be happier than many children today who have a house full of toys. We didn't think of ourselves as poor or underprivileged or anything like that, because most people around us were in the same boat.

I always was fond of eating, and so my fondest childhood memories of Christmas involve Mamma's cooking. Christmas

Eve was a fasting day for Catholics—no meat or big meals on that day. About ten o'clock we left home for Midnight Mass at East Margaree on the woodsleigh pulled by Ida, our brown mare. The sleigh was boarded up on each side, and straw was put down in the wagon for us. There was a board across the front for the driver to sit on. Most of the time, Papa took us, because Mamma was too busy getting the food ready at home.

It took about an hour or a little more to get there, and the neighbours would visit a bit before the Mass. The Mass itself took about two hours because of all the special services for Christmas, and then another hour to get home. It was around three a.m. before we were home again, cold and hungry as bears, and there was a great big feed all ready for us. I can't think of anything more pleasurable in life to a boy than coming in from the cold and dark to Mamma's warm kitchen full of delicious smells.

My mother made "isbean" months before Christmas, a kind of sausage pudding in casings—these were familiar to Scottish people. The sausages were made of beef, suet, onions, and oats, and they were highly seasoned. The casings were the intestines of the animal, and they were thoroughly cleaned before they were filled and sealed at both ends. Each sausage was two or three inches in diameter and a foot and a half long and they were hung in loops in the attic to age. Some people fried them, but my mother boiled them, puncturing the casings. Then she cut them up in three-inch chunks and served them steaming hot with all the potatoes we could eat.

But we were careful to save enough room for the mince pies. Mamma's huge basin heaped with mincemeat was stored in a cool place until she was ready to make the pies. I can almost taste that mincemeat now—it was spicy and tangy, a lot better than the canned stuff you buy in the stores now. She also made another special treat—homemade raisin loaf with molasses. She managed to make it so that it raised light and fine, not heavy like some other women made it. To us it was manna from heaven.

People tended to come in and out all day between Christmas and New Year's, and there was always food and fiddling. Johnny Steven White was the one who first taught my brother Angus and me quite a number of fiddle tunes, and I learned to chord on the guitar with a steel Hawaiian slide to keep time with Angus.

Other fiddle players visited our place, like Hughie Angus Lord MacDonald, Ronald Gillis, Angus Allan Gillis. We were exposed to quite a number of really good musicians. Gaelic singers came over too now and then, like the MacFarlanes from South West Margaree, John P. Chisholm and his mother. Then my mother liked to sing along in the chorus. She had a very lovely voice, but she rarely sang except in private as she went about her work, particularly her spinning. Her foot would be going up and down the paddle of the small wheel and she would sing songs in Gaelic. Two of her favourites were "The High Road to Linton" and "Lame Malcolm of the Glen" both of which have many verses. Because of her, all of us knew a great many Gaelic tunes by ear. I think my father went through agony and sometimes wished that the fiddle Angus and I had was in kindling wood for the stove. The fiddle strings weren't good, the bridge was sometimes a crude homemade thing, but we figured if it was a fiddle we ought to be able to get tunes out of it. We were noisy, and not very good musicians in those years. But gradually, we learned the tunes properly and improved, and then there was always music when we were home.

Tom Chisholm from Antigonish married in Margaree and became manager of the creamery. When he was in World War I, he became friends with Sydney Oland of Oland's Brewery. On two occasions, Tom took Colonel Oland down to the house to hear some fiddle music, and as soon as the neighbours got wind of it, they all landed at Archie Chisholm's for entertainment.

Perhaps many people today would pity us because we were so poor, and I know some people my age who are embarrassed to talk about hardships and how little of the world's goods they possessed in those years. But not me. I wouldn't change one bit of it. We had family, lots of good neighbours, and life was full of spice.

Christmas Trouble

Brenda Sampson

My poor parents. I don't know how they did it! I'm sure they no sooner got to bed when we'd get up around one on Christmas morning. We would run to the tree, shrieking with excitement to see what Santa brought us. There's nothing like shaking a present and hearing it make noise to set your mind wondering wshat it is.

This happened to me one Christmas when I was in elementary school. The pretty gift I picked up made a ton of noise! I was so excited! I opened it to reveal a game. Two, three or four people could play this memorable board game with the fun centre piece! It looked like a lot of fun and naturally I wanted to play it right away! My exhausted parents convinced me to wait until later that morning.

The moment I woke up for the second time I ran to my new game. It wasn't long before my sister Gina and I were having fun playing the game. It was called *Trouble*. It certainly was noisy, but we didn't mind. We played this game all day! We loved it! We ate our lunch—we called it dinner then—and then our supper—not wasting a moment to get back at the game and ignoring our father's repeated suggestions to "Please give it a break."

By the time it was early evening, our father had had enough of this noisy game. He was the one who needed a break. As it was Christmas Day, he didn't want to upset me by taking away my cherished present; so, he made me an offer. The man was a stellar salesman, so I didn't stand a chance! He offered me one dollar if I stopped playing the game for one hour. Now, one dollar could buy a lot in the 1970s and I was no fool—so of course, I accepted the deal.

Now, when you're in elementary school, an hour can seem like an eternity. It was hard to stop looking at the clock. Finally, time was up—and my sister and I resumed playing that noisy game until we had to go to bed because we were so tired. I'm sure my parents regretted giving me this game for Christmas, but it is one of my favourite memories!

Many years later, as an adult, I gave my parents a special Christmas gift. I made them wait until all the other presents had been opened. Well, to their surprise, there it was again! A brand new version of the game of *Trouble*. They laughed and shouted and started to recount the story of a memorable Christmas Day, many years ago. And yes, I made them play the game.

Once Upon a Christmas Eve

Leonard Eckhaus

This is based on a true story about how my wife Linda and I, along with two complete strangers—two Jewish, two Christian—each with their own compelling need to get home to their families for Christmas, shared in a bit of magic, an enchanted moment, all on a Christmas Eve many years ago.

On Christmas Eve, December 24th, 2006, my wife Linda and I were booked on a six p.m. flight to return home to Las Vegas from Orange County, California, where we had spent the last week celebrating Hanukkah with our children and grandchildren. It was the airline's last flight of the day.

Little did we realize that we were about to embark upon what would become for the four of us involved, a magical Christmas experience, worthy of a Hallmark TV movie.

As we sat at the gate, waiting to board, we got into a conversation with a young man in an army uniform. His name was Darren and he was on his way home to Virginia. He had a connecting flight at midnight in Las Vegas to get him there. He was quite excited as he explained that he had just completed boot camp and was on his way home to spend Christmas Day with his family before being shipped out overseas the very next day.

His face lit up as he told us that his girlfriend would also be there, and he planned on proposing to her. He had wrapped her ring to look just like any other Christmas present and was going to put it under their tree and watch her unwrap it. You could see just how excited he was as he took the ring out of his duffel bag and showed it to us. It was wrapped in Christmas paper.

As we were sitting there, I noticed the flight board began flashing "cancelled" next to our flight.

I jumped up and was the first person to get to the lady behind the desk to find out what was going on. I was told that there was a mechanical problem with the plane and that they had to fly the part they needed in from another airport, but it wouldn't get there until sometime the next day.

She said that they were going to bus everyone on this flight to Los Angeles International Airport where they would get us all on a flight from there, very early the next morning.

I went back to Linda and told her the news. We decided that we would simply hire a limo to drive us back to Las Vegas. It would be expensive but it beat hanging around the airport in Los Angeles all night.

We had a good friend, Tommy, who owned Exotic Limousines in Orange County and I called him, but he told me that on such short notice and because it was Christmas Eve, he had no way of finding a driver, especially to go all the way to Las Vegas and back. After I begged him to try, he said he would make a few calls, but he didn't have much hope.

My cell phone rang about ten minutes later. It was Tommy. "I have somebody," he said, "but it is going to be expensive."

I didn't even ask how much. I simply replied, "How soon can he get here?" It was now six-thirty and he said the car and driver could be there by seven.

Linda and I decided to ask the young soldier who needed to make the connection in Las Vegas, if he would like to come with us. It would be tight for him to make his midnight connection, but we had a chance. And when I asked him, the look of his disappointment in not being able to get home in time, instantly changed into a broad smile. He couldn't thank us enough.

Feeling good about helping him, we sat back in our seats and waited for the limo.

As fate would have it, as we were waiting, we ended up in a conversation with a young woman named Laura, whose Dad had passed away just two weeks before. She was also desperate to get to Las Vegas this evening. Because it was Christmas and so close to her father's death, she didn't want her mother to wake up alone on Christmas morning.

So, for the second time that evening, we asked another stranger if she would like to join us, along with the soldier, on our journey.

This was becoming a real adventure. Complete strangers, all caught up in the magical spirit of Christmas Eve. And our destinies were, whether we realized it or not, now forever linked.

The limo arrived a few minutes past seven and we quickly got in, anxious to begin our journey. As I looked at my watch, I remember thinking that with any luck we could get to the Las Vegas airport between eleven and eleven thirty, just in time for Darren's midnight connection.

We sat huddled together in the rear of the limo, Linda and I in the very back seat, facing Darren and Laura. In the door panels we could see bottles of water and some snacks. There was also a bottle of champagne in a bucket filled with ice.

I loosened the scarf I was wearing but left my coat on. Linda unbuttoned her jacket and we all settled in, making ourselves as comfortable as we could.

Huddled together, across from each other, no one said anything for the next few minutes, waiting for the car to warm up.

Once we were underway and as the temperature got more comfortable, Darren thanked us for bringing him along and helping him make his connection. Then he told us that he had never been in a limo before. "I never thought I'd be in a limousine," he said. "These are for movie stars and important people."

He went on to tell us that he had grown up in Lexington, Virginia. His father worked as a janitor at the Washington and Lee University and his mom was a waitress at a local restaurant. They had both graduated high school but neither attended college. He had two younger sisters, Mary Rose and Karen. The family struggled financially, and Darren always had some kind of job for as far back as he could remember, doing chores for neighbours when he was very young and then working as a handyman when he was old enough. He told us that he was good at fixing things.

After he graduated high school, he immediately enlisted in the army, and he was excited about being sent to Germany.

He told us that his girlfriend, Julie, was a high school senior and they had been together since they met four years ago. She wanted to go to college and become a nurse.

I remember thinking about how young he was and how he and Julie were just beginning their lives and had so much to look forward to. I thought back to Linda and I when we were just dating and I was a little bit jealous of Darren.

I told them that Linda and I met when we were both twelve years old and that we began dating when we had just turned seventeen. We were married when we were nineteen and had been married for forty-four years.

"Well," he said, looking around the limo, "it looks like you did pretty well."

"We've been fortunate," I responded, "but it wasn't always like this." "And believe me," Linda added, "there were lots of bumps in the road."

Laura told us that she had been seeing someone for almost a year now, but she still wasn't sure he was the one with whom she wanted to spend the rest of her life. "He was very caring when my father died last month," she said, "but when I told him I was going to Las Vegas to be with my mom over Christmas, he decided to stay in California and celebrate the holiday with his family. I'm really disappointed that he won't be with me in Las Vegas. He knows how much my mom really needs me this year."

We spent the next few hours learning a lot about each other and the more we shared about our lives, the closer we began to feel. And before long we each realized that we had all made new friends for life.

When we entered the Las Vegas city limits, I opened the bottle of champagne, and we toasted the spirits that had brought us together on this one special evening.

We arrived at the Las Vegas airport at eleven-thirty, just in time for Darren to make his connection. Then we took Laura to her mom's.

On the way to our own home, Linda and I both felt that our evening had truly been surreal, and that we had just been part of something very, very special.

The magic of that Christmas Eve, along with the memory of strangers who needed each other, found each other, and embarked on a journey of love together. While it was just for that one day— we never met again—it will always be with us.

The Pre-Christmas Gift

Kay Globe

It was a day in early December 2022 that I was shopping at the grocery store in Sydney. I only went in for a few items, but decided to try and pick up some of my Christmas groceries before the rush started. After I picked up some groceries I proceeded to the cashier.

As I was standing in line with my groceries I looked behind me. A gentleman was behind me. I noticed that he only had one item in his hand.

I turned and told him he could go ahead of me. He replied, "Really?" I said, "Yes, I am not in a hurry."

The cashier started to ring his order. I started to put my order on the counter and as I did she started to ring it in with his. I politely told her that that was my order, not the gentleman's. She replied that the gentleman said he was paying for my groceries.

I was in shock. I told him he did not have to do that but he said he wanted to because I was kind to him. He did not want any fanfare and wished me a Merry Christmas, paid $150-plus for the groceries and left the store.

What a nice gesture from a complete stranger. In return I offered many prayers for him—and still do.

I Remember the Gift

The Rev. Gordon Cann

Lorena Forbrigger called in a book order and we went on to discuss Christmas stories. She had one that was part of a letter a minister had sent her; it was on her fridge about twenty years. She read it aloud and we recorded it over the phone—a lovely, painful story.

On one side of the letter, Rev. Cann had written, "Christmas is the time of the year we often think of those who are very special to us, those we haven't seen for a while, and those whose company we often enjoyed throughout the year. At this time more than at any other, we like to let them know that we are thinking of them in the warmest way. And because you are among these special people, I just thought you should know you are thought of very warmly, not just at Christmas but at many times throughout the year."

In the back of the letter Rev. Cann offered this story from his childhood. He called it "I Remember the Gift."

I remember December 7th, 1941. I was seven years old. That was the day Pearl Harbour was bombed. I don't remember that. But that Sunday evening I printed my name on the Christmas card that I was giving my friends at school, while my mother wrote notes on Christmas cards. It was a happy evening.

What happened the next morning would cast a shadow over the Christmas celebrations of my youth. Our minister arrived as I was finishing breakfast. He had a telegram from Ottawa. Ronald, my oldest brother, had been killed overseas.

I didn't go to school that day. At recess there would be a practice for our Christmas Pageant. I was a shepherd, and I didn't want to miss it. Just before recess, the teacher asked me to stay behind. She told me that she knew I would be too sad to be in the pageant and she had given that part to someone else. Well, that really made me sad.

But there was still the Sunday School concert. I was the "A" in C-H-R-I-S-T-M-A-S. I would hold up a large "A" card and I would say clearly, slowly and loudly: "A is for Angels whose voices rang: 'Good will and peace on earth. Thank God.'"

That evening my Sunday School teacher came to the house for the cake. As she was leaving, she whispered to me, "Everyone knows your house is in mourning over Ronald. So I'm going to find someone else to do your part. And you won't have to come to practice in Calvin Hall any more."

She smiled at me and I tried to smile back. Her cake had bright pink strawberry-flavoured icing.

The years have passed, and cake—strawberry-flavoured anything—still nauseates me.

We never went to the Christmas concerts because—we were too sad to go to places like that.

And I did get a big bag of hard candy. My friend, Edison, asked Santa Claus at the Sunday School concert for an extra bag.

And I asked my mother about a Christmas tree and my mother told me it would not be right to have a tree and put up decorations, because Ronald was dead.

"Is Sanda Claus going to stay away from our sad house too?" I asked my mother.

"No. He will come."

"But where will he put the presents, if we don't have a tree?"

My mother hesitated, and then she replied: "Oh, he'll probably put them at the end of your bed."

My other brother, seeing my sad face, asked if he could have a small tree for my bedroom. My mother agreed to a small tree. "But it will have to go out as soon as the needles begin to drop."

It was a beautiful tree—all my own! And I wasn't allowed to show it to anyone. Or tell anyone.

On Christmas Eve my parents were surprised by a visit from Mr. and Mrs. Hiltz. She was the second Mrs. Hiltz, and had never been to our house before. She had come from up in Nova Scotia and had a reputation for being distant and a severe stepmother. People like my mother who had been friends of the first Mrs. Hiltz, kept their distance.

I used to visit the second Mrs. Hiltz with some of my friends. My mother tried to discourage my visits because she felt I might be a nuisance and get in trouble—and she didn't want to "cross swords with that woman."

Mrs. Hiltz was carrying a large parcel. Mrs. Hiltz said the parcel was for me. Because I was such a pleasant child and she enjoyed my visits.

My parents were surprised. And pleased.

Later, my father said to me, "That gift is a great compliment for you, and for our family." And he smiled.

I had not seen that smile since we heard about my brother's death.

The gift was a wind-up train. It had real cars and tracks.

Later, as I lay in bed listening to Christmas carols on the radio downstairs, I noticed moonlight shining through the frost on my window. In the frost I saw the shapes of angels, and I said to myself, "A is for Angels whose voices rang 'Good will and peace on earth' they sang." And the beautiful peace seemed to settle on our sad house. And I went to sleep thinking of the wonderful gift I had received downstairs, and the wonderful smile on my father's face.

The Snowless Christmas, 1984

Elena LeBlanc

It was near Christmas in 1984 and it was very hot and we were the only white people. The others who were brown-skinned would exclaim at the sight of us, and my mother says they would pick me up without asking and bring me to show their family the little white girl with my mother running behind to catch up and not lose me.

The air was hot and heavy and always the same. People in North America often make small talk about the weather but in places where the weather is always the same no one says "nice day today" or comments on the lack of clouds in the clear sky. Instead they talk about the things they dreamed or the things they want to do. As the world becomes more and more consumeristic the small talk has morphed into people speaking of the things they bought or the things they will buy; but in 1984 life was more simple in this underdeveloped place. There were huge lizards everywhere and they would make a low-tone sound: "uck-oo" "uck-oo" all the time . . . .

The bugs were massive too, and it was quite funny to observe the reactions of some of the ladies to a critter that had crawled into her shoe during the night. We always had to shake out our shoes before putting them on and I still do it now, even here in Nova Scotia, so many years later.

But let us go back in time now to long ago . . . and here we are in this faraway place and it is Christmastime; but there is no tree and no lights and no holiday carols permeating the silence at every turn. Instead we see barefoot parentless children living in cardboard boxes, scrounging for food in the trash. All the food there was so spicy. You could not buy food (except fruit) that was bland—all was heavily spiced. We had to boil the water and the milk for at least ten minutes and I really did not like the taste of the powdered milk; so my mother would put raisins in my cup that I could eat if I drank the milk first. It was a game for me to drink the gross white stuff until I could start to see the little mounds of dark dried fruit at the bottom of the cup. Such unspeakable joy for that little girl, when finally the gross white liquid was done, and she could just eat the sweet dried grapes.

Yes that sun was very very hot! On one hot day my mother came across what she thought was a swimming pool. She took me into the cool water and was teaching me to swim when suddenly the entire town was there pointing and laughing. We were swimming in the village water supply! At least they had a sense of humour about it and thought it was the funniest thing they ever saw—the white lady and little girl were swimming in the drinking water. For some reason they thought that since we were white-skinned that we were cleaner than them . . . but we weren't.

Merry Christmas! . . . and that two-year-old me was so excited in a way that only the very young and the very old can appreciate. I remember I asked my mother why she wasn't excited about it and she said that she had already lived so many Christmases, that it just wasn't special for her anymore. So I made the decision that it must be quite unpleasant to be a grown-up.

I decided that I would refuse to become a big person who didn't get excited about things anymore. If only I could have kept that resolution. In some ways I suppose that I have. I mean, in 2020 when the Covid Virus shut everything down worldwide, my children and I celebrated a full-on Christmas in May 2020. There is even a photograph of all of us piled into one kayak going down the river that runs through the little town of Antigonish.

I will finish this typing about the 1984 memories with my breakfast on Christmas Morning! Pancakes! There was a man who would make them and my mother paid him to make one for me and set me up at a little table on the veranda outside the house we were renting. I felt like a princess!

Then this big black raven or crow flew down and landed on the other side of the veranda, CAW-CAWing and looking at me. What a glorious bird! In my adult life I read in Greek legends about how the ravens came to be: According to the long ago story, it was a white dove that was carrying a Message of Love, but then some character (perhaps one of the ancient made-up gods) felt jilted and made a fire and burned the houses of the family that they were upset with. The dove with the Love Message escaped the flames, but all that smoke turned its white feathers to black. That is how the Raven came to be a black bird instead of a white bird, the mourning dove.

Anyway, there I was on the veranda and this bird landed some paces away and was looking at me. So I got up from my seat and walked closer to it. Then behind me, another bird swooped down and took my pancake! It landed on the rooftop of the house next door and both birds proceeded to share my breakfast pancake, laughing at me in their CAW-CAWing for falling for their trick and stealing my food. Oh how I cried! But my mother simply paid the man to make me another one and instructed me to not let the birds trick me again . . . not even if a dozen birds landed near me! She used to say:

"You can't keep the birds from flying over your head, but you don't have to let them build a nest in your head, or on your bed!"

And so I end this story now with another bird-related quote, which just so happens to be the funniest insult that I have ever heard in my entire life! So, if you are someone who doesn't like me and wishes harm upon me or my family and friends, then please know that I pray for you every day.

In the spirit of kindness and forgiveness I dedicate this insult to you, my enemy, in the hopes that you turn away from your hatred. You can choose today to leave the past behind and live for goodness and truth; now in this present moment you have a present under your life tree . . . here and now is my Christmas Gift to you:

"May the droppings of a thousand sparrows forever be upon your head."

When I pray for you, my enemy, I pray for you to have peace. I pray for you to be lifted out of your pain.

May joy overflow your life with Hope, Love, and the Fireworks of the New Year that will come days after all the presents have been opened. We can curl up with a cup of hot milk by the fireplace, no matter how old and wrinkly we become. Like a raisin left out in the sun too long. We can still choose to be sweet.

The Hockey Gloves

Randall James

Flipping through the Canadian Tire catalogue, my eyes fell upon the Toronto Maple Leafs "pro-style" hockey gloves with the cool "V" design. I desperately wanted them. In fact, I wanted everything "Leafs." The blue-and-white gloves were thick and well-padded and I knew they would feel great when I gripped my hockey stick.

I also put the Leafs hockey jersey on my wish list. It was a couple of weeks before Christmas 1971, and this ten-year-old worshipped star centre, Dave Keon, and all the Leaf players. I just had to get those gloves.

I got my love of hockey from my dad, whom we had left two years before in London, Ontario. My older sister Alison and I had been collected by my mother years after she had abandoned us. That's how we ended up in scenic Cape Breton. We had been kind of like orphans for the first eight years of life, bouncing from house to house under my irresponsible father.

My new family lived on the hill at the top of White's Lane, Low Point, where we had a great view of the ocean over the snow-covered birch trees. Low Point was situated about half way between Sydney and New Waterford, just off the main highway. Our small white cottage, with black trim, had a coal stove in the kitchen, and my older brother Bradley and I were responsible for going out to the barn and collecting coal and firewood every couple of days.

Each morning, wearing two sweaters over our pajamas and two pairs of socks, we huddled around that black stove as Ma got the fire going. A full tree stood in the corner of the living room decorated with gold and silver tinsel garlands and ball ornaments, and Christmas cards sat upon the stereo console.

That Christmas, Low Point was a winter wonderland, and Petrie's Lake, located two hundred yards behind our house, was frozen over. While the boys played games of shinny hockey, the girls figure skated at various spots across the huge ice surface. The lake was so large that there were multiple games of hockey going on at the same time. One scary thing about Petrie's Lake was seeing the dark spots under the ice and once in a while hearing a loud CRRAAAACCK sound and having the fear in the back of your mind that you might fall through.

In fact, Ma did fall in one year, but it was very close to the edge so the freezing water only reached to her waist, and Johnny, who had been checking the ice thickness with an axe, was able to get her out. Johnny, who was about ten years older than Ma, was our new step-dad and a pretty good guy. I got along with him well, most likely because I was nice to his son Junior, who was four years younger than I.

Bradley, two-and-a-half years older than I, whom I had also

just met when we moved down, was a great skater, and of course, a Montreal Canadiens fan. (Brothers are born for adversity they say.) He was a left-handed shooter, while I shot right. I was lanky and skated on my ankles, which I attributed to old and soft second-hand skates, which I seemed to always own through the years. Being a younger brother I often got hand-me-downs. Early on Christmas morning, my siblings and I woke up like all the kids in Cape Breton, with joyful anticipation. We raced into the living room and ripped through our presents. There were standard family gifts like *Spirograph* and *Trouble*, books, socks and clothing items, but my heart was set on those gloves.

Searching, I found a present with my name on it and the right size. I opened it and . . . and it was a pair of blue-and-white hockey gloves with a small Maple Leafs logo on each one. But these were obviously not the "pro-style" gloves. No, these were the cheapo version. They were thin and stiff, and the wrist protection part was made out of plastic. The blue colour was not Maple Leafs blue at all. The disappointment. Ugh. I crammed my hands into the tight gloves but there was hardly room for my fingers. Great.

Realizing that Ma was watching, I caught myself and pretended to like them. I don't know if depression was written all over my face, but I felt like crying. The only good thing was that I was still expecting one other gift—a Leafs hockey sweater.

I soon found another box with my name and opened it. The jersey, if you could call it a jersey, was solid blue with white patches above the shoulder area—and no Maple Leafs logo. Great. Once again, Ma and Johnny had gone cheap. Adding to my misery was the fact that Bradley owned a real Canadiens jersey.

That was such a heart-breaking Christmas. Looking back, I had no idea that Christmases would go downhill from there. (And was it just a coincidence that the Habs would dominate the 1970s, winning six Stanley Cups while my beloved Leafs would get so bad that disgruntled fans would end up wearing paper bags over their heads?) Good grief, as that other lovable loser, Charlie Brown, might say.

The next eight years, especially now that Ma decided to leave Johnny and move to New Waterford, a small coal-mining town, were going to be "skinny" years of poverty and scraping by. Our family's lack of finances was often highlighted during Christmas. Of course, we could always depend on Nana giving us two dollars in a Christmas card with all the important words underlined (once or twice for emphasis) and a book of Life Savers candies.

The poverty issues spilled into all my hockey dreams—and they were big. For the first few years in New Waterford, I played goaltender in the minor hockey system, which was the perfect position for me because I got free goalie gear. It was not mine to take home, of course. I just had to show up early before each game and they gave me the equipment. Somehow, though, I always got a stiff catching glove that never opened or closed properly, making it difficult to catch pucks with.

Nevertheless, I did well and made the all-star team one year. The only part of the gear that I had to provide was a pair of skates and a cup—which I absolutely did not have. Just before one game, the coach skated up to me and asked me if I had my cup on. "Yeah," I said, as he poked me with his stick at the same time to make sure. Thankfully he missed.

In '75, we moved again, within New Waterford, this time to the Low Rentals duplexes on Hudson Street close to the ocean. The writing was on the wall as to my future wealth.

Alison ran away back to Ontario in '75 and Bradley left for the Navy in '76. I stuck it out until Grade 12—winning the chess championship that year. A few weeks after graduating from Breton Education Centre in '79, I was on a train to join the military so that I could send money home to Ma, as Bradley was doing. I joined the Air Force and became an instrument tech on fighter jets and was posted to West Germany. At least now I was able to afford a few nice things, like Nike sneakers and cool leather jackets.

The Hockey Gloves

After leaving the Air Force, I settled in Calgary, working for Field Aviation at the airport repairing aircraft. I got married to Katie, who I had met in Germany, and we had two wonderful boys. I became a big Flames fan and got to attend a few games. One of those was against my beloved Leafs. It was a dream to watch them play live, but my heart was now split between these two teams.

I took my two-year-old son Jason to a Flames game, and I remember that we got Casey, his younger brother, a Flames shirt. During the Flames march to the Stanley Cup in '89 I bought myself a Flames jersey and would often look down and caress the large flaming "C" crest.

I developed a good friendship with Bryan, a fellow tech and mentor, and he invited me to join a group of guys from work playing rec hockey at a local arena on Fridays at midnight. I didn't own any equipment, so went to Sport Chek and bought a new hockey stick, gloves and skates. Bryan told me he had an extra helmet that I could use.

On a frigid night in January 1990, Bryan picked me up, and we drove to the arena. The helmet fit well and the black-and-white Cooper gloves were top-notch quality. It was so nice, for the first time in my life, to grip a hockey stick with that real feel. The first night on the ice I was surprised that I was a pretty good skater and could easily keep up with the action.

On one play, I had a breakaway on the goaltender who I decked out, but slid a backhand pass to Bryan, who fired the puck into an empty net. We were just like kids.

On another chance to score, I rifled the puck off the cross-bar and in. I can still remember how great it felt to shoot with those gloves. With my size and strength, I realized that I had advantages over the other players, but it was only rec hockey and any dreams of playing pro were long gone.

Through the years, as we get older and look back at those precious childhood memories, what helps us to overcome any bitterness or resentment, like disappointing Christmas gifts? For me, the answer is in the famous words that Linus taught Charlie Brown, and all of us, about what Christmas is all about.

It's a lot about Grace.

Maybe the "pro-style" gloves were too expensive that year. Maybe Ma and Johnny were worried about having two extra mouths to feed. We have to look back on life with grace, especially when we become parents and spouses and see that we also make mistakes—sometimes big ones.

I'm sixty years old now and have lived in Victoria for over twenty years. I still keep an eye on the Leafs, who have a great team and a real shot to win the cup for the first time since '67. Who knows, I still might get those Maple Leaf gloves after all.

The Christmas Tree Dentist

Jitka Zgola

This was the year I planned to overcome my dread of singing solo and just do it! I'd been singing with the church choir for several years now and felt pretty good as a soprano. But I had never had the nerve to volunteer for a solo part on Christmas Eve. This year, though, I had done it, I had raised my hand when our choir mistress asked for solo volunteers, and she gave me a spot.

Over the two months before Christmas, I really practiced. I was ready . . . until . . . just three days before Christmas, at the office party, as I bit into a crispy wedge of apple, I felt that awful snap. A front tooth had broken totally off its post.

The Christmas Tree Dentist

"Thit!" I thputtered. "There goeth my thuper plan to thing tholo with the choir on Chrithmath Eve! How can I thing 'Thilent Night' mithing a front tooth? Thit, thit, thit. Well, at leatht I can thpout the word, thit, without rethervathon. That'th one thing you can do when you're mithng a front tooth."

But, really, what to do? It was a wonderful relief when my Christmas angel dentist found me a spot in his schedule and agreed to do an emergency repair the very next morning.

"The Christmas spirit is alive and well!" I thought. "My solo performance is saved!"

Until, that is, the next afternoon, the day of Christmas Eve . . . . We were setting up the tree we had cut down in the woods, a lovely little spruce, all full and fresh. We had just paused to have a little toddy, and I'd no sooner raised my glass to my mouth when I felt a tooth floating loose along with my first sip of warm spicy rum.

"Oh thit!" I thputtered again, totally devathtated. "Now my hopeth of thinging are thuper thot. No-one'th going to fixth thith tooth now!" And slapped my hand against my thigh . . . . where it stuck.

A gob of spruce resin, that had attached itself to my jeans as we brought the tree into the house, was now smudged and gluing my hand down firmly and giving me another opportunity to use my new-found free expletive. Everything was going wrong. Now the tree would be dropping sticky resin all over the living room.

"Careful with that thap," I called to everyone. "It won't come off of anything. It'th a thuperglue!"

" . . . and a super antibiotic," chimed in my eagle scout son. "It's been used to fill up dental cavities and heal wounds. And, hey . . . . "

He didn't get a chance to finish his sentence as we were all seized by the same idea. I found a nice firm little ball of sap that had oozed from the bark of our Christmas tree and firmed up a bit. I then dried the gap in my front teeth as much as I could, pressed the resin ball into the space and pushed the broken tooth back where it belonged. It stayed and it stayed well.

I did sing my solo on Christmas Eve. With great gusto, exuberance and no lisp.

It held for several days. I saw the New Year in with a little bit of sap handy for the occasional fix. Tomorrow, I have an appointment for my permanent repair. I wonder what my dentist will say when he notices a wad of spruce resin in the place of the dental cement he had used.

That little bit of sap was my best Christmas present, delivered by the Christmas tree dentist.

The First Goose of Christmas

Gary LeDrew

Jill was a model. She was long and lovely with smooth skin, bright hazel eyes and bobbed hair that seemed long out of date but it worked on her. She was one of the naturals. She had a magical metabolism that allowed her to eat and drink like a normal person and her only exercise was a couple of daily walks with her westie Cindy Lou. Well, sort of her dog. Cindy had come with her new husband a couple of years before. He being a Scot, a Glasgow Keelie even, and somehow William Kylie MacDougall had grown up into a brilliant movie producer/writer. He even thought of himself as a bit of a big fish in a small pond in the Canadian Movie Business and in Toronto carried himself with just enough arrogance to be acceptable in Toronto society. He had the touch of that almost mystic ability to attract money and

The First Goose of Christmas

models. He had met Jill at the Mirvish Benefit for the Arts. At first a conquest, they were soon an item. They dated for a year and to everyone's surprise got married.

Now in the second year of marriage they were delighted how comfortable and domestic their situation had become. Well, except for the cooking. Jill wasn't a great cook so they went out a lot, which suited their style. Their friends and confrères frequented the Windsor Arms, and the three restaurants there afforded convenience and enough variety to make them popular regulars. Jill was able to fix breakfast, build the odd stew, and even a roast beef and a chop weren't completely beyond her. But mostly they went out except for Sundays and special occasions which helped demonstrate some domestication.

Their first Christmas was saved with a phone call to her mother in Calgary who went through the steps of cooking the turkey clearly and concisely. It had been a moderate success. Bill especially liked the bacon on the breast to keep it moist. Like most Scots he had a passion for bacon and it more or less made the meal for him. Jill had hoped for more enthusiasm which wasn't forthcoming, but at least it was never one of his criticisms either.

The goose had come up over cocktails at the 22. They were doubling with Bill's buddy Cyrill Beacom, a fellow Scot who had emigrated into the Canadian Film Board, and his girlfriend of long standing, Margo. All three had broken the Martini rule: "One is not enough and three is too many." When somehow with a flitting reminiscence of Scottish Christmases of long ago, there was a mention of the custom of the goose for dinner and the callow Canadian custom of the common turkey. Jill, almost finishing the third martini, graciously or condescendingly— depending on your take—made the invitation, said: "Okay. Christmas dinner at our place—and I'm cooking a goose."

The goose was no problem. She ordered it at St. Lawrence Market and picked it up the day before Xmas, fresh-killed, plump and plucked, and the biggest she could get. She bought all her

Christmas supplies there, homemade chestnut stuffing ready for the bird, cranberry relish, little red potatoes, little carrots and waxed turnips—he liked to call them neeps like Bill did—and of course thick slices of prime bacon. It was a great goose and she thrilled with anticipation of the joy it would bring to her emigrant Scottish husband and his friend. Christmas Morning had turned into a bit of a lie-in after a night out with a bit too much Chardonnay.

But she arose bright-eyed bravely at noon—she was always bright-eyed—if not bushy-tailed—to face the goose. It was big. It had taken serious rearranging to fit it into the fridge. But she was brave. She had faced a thousand runways and won the day and a bloody goose wasn't going to defeat her. She cleaned and washed it and stuffed it like the turkey. She made slits in the breast skin and threaded through the nice fat bacon slices. It didn't matter that the bird didn't fit in the roasting pan because it didn't fit in the oven either.

So she walked Cindy Lou and wondered, and when she returned she looked at the clock, opened a bottle of Chardonnay, poured herself a glass and was assessing the situation when Margo came by to lend a hand.

It had only taken Margo half a glass to find the answer. "The Barbeque," said Margo.

They were still living in Bill's apartment, one of the Renos just off West Bloor, the upper half of a house on a nicely treed street. It was not exactly trendy but nice enough—a roomy two-bedroom, a large living room and a small but private wooden enclosed patio.

Time was a wasting and they moved quickly. In fur coats and long stylish boots, they surveyed the barbeque. It was perfect, easily big enough. There was a rotisserie in the large lid and lots of gas; it was barely used.

They removed the cover, broke it free from the ice and dragged it to the door. There wasn't enough room between the steps and the fence with ice and snow, and she didn't want to traipse through the snow and have to put her long boots on each time she went out. So, with further cleverness, she pulled the front wheels up the first step and hung the barbeque at an angle; it held nicely in place with the butcher's string tied to a post. They mounted the bird, lit the fire, closed the lid, and plugged in the rotisserie and turned it on. They stepped back and admired the inspiration and retired to the kitchen to open another bottle of Chardonnay.

It was about an hour later when the sound of sirens reminded them to check on the bird. They opened the door and saw the carnage through the smoke about the same time the firemen arrived. In the aftermath the fire chief reconstructed the incident: When the bird started cooking the skin shrunk a bit which let loose a slice of bacon which plopped down and flopped around a few times before it acted like a wick taking the fire up to plump greasy breast of the bird which set it ablaze like a napalm bomb and in turn set fire to the string which burnt away and, leaving the barbeque to fall over into the patio fence and burn it pretty well to the floor of the patio. The firemen arrived in time to save the house and except for a huge expensive mess and a ruined dinner, things weren't terrible, only bad . . . .

It was a good thing they were regulars at the Courtyard Café because a simple phone call got them a table right away for a gourmet turkey dinner. Jill was nearly inconsolable but another bottle of Chardonnay cheered her up and if the Scots didn't get their goose dinner they got a pretty good dinner and a great after-dinner story known as the "Napalm Goose" and, in their business, that is just about as good.

Angels in the Story

Minerva MacInnis

This marvelous woman will be my sister-friend forever. She is a loving, giving and wise person who knows and accepts my/her family as we are. Beautiful inside and out, she radiates and personifies the love of God. Her laughter is infectious.

The first Christmas she found herself alone with three young children, she lived in a small top-floor apartment up a steep set of stairs in Sydney. We knew her home was brimming with the spirit of Christmas, with love and humour. Money not so much.

On the other hand here we were with our daughter J and her friend R, Christmas shopping with abandon and without concern about our grocery money. We always enjoyed time spent together with these two girls because they were full of fun, energy, and contagious laughter. We hatched a plan.

We shopped—for a laundry basket! We filled it randomly to overflowing with everything from postage stamps to envelopes, candy to aspirin, shampoo to body cream, laundry and dish soap, gift cards to wrapping paper . . . . You get the picture.

The crowning cumbersome jewels were the oversized packages of toilet paper and paper towels.

This shopping spree, two or three days before Christmas about twenty-two years ago, was joyful, fun and exciting. We stopped the car down the block, sending the girls laughing and laden down with the basket and jewels for delivery. They made their way as quietly as possible. At the top of the dark narrow stairway, they piled the loot, knocked and ran!

My sister-friend later told me about the Angels who showed

up—that day, and a few more Christmases after. Of being stuck behind the parcels and never able to catch them. But of hearing their pounding footsteps and fading giggles as they ran away.

The Teddy Bear

Jane Monaghan

My maternal grandmother was born in Newfoundland in the early 1900s and lived there until the age of sixteen. She left to seek employment in Cape Breton. There she met and married a lovely man (also from Newfoundland) and had two girls, both who became nurses. One of these was my mother.

When my grandmother was in her early 70s, she was living by herself after my grandfather had passed away. I would go often to visit her and we would have long conversations. Once I asked her what it was like growing up in Newfoundland, especially at Christmastime. She said she grew up in a family of ten children. There was very little money as her father fished from a company schooner and could be gone for months at a time. The money he earned was mostly owed to the company store, and there would be very little left over after the debts to the store were paid.

She said Christmas was a happy time as her father would be home with the family. Christmas dinner was always a goose (turkey was unheard-of at that time) and lots of vegetables from the family garden. The vegetables were stored in a root cellar to last the winter and there were always plenty. For dessert the family would have a pie or a raisin cake, all made by the mother and older girls.

She said her father and brothers would go to the woods to get a tree and it would be put up in the parlour. The parlour would only be used for special occasions in those days. The children would make decorations out of coloured paper and take turns decorating the tree. Long paper chains and snowflake cut-outs filled the tree. Small real candles were also on the tree but were rarely lit as her mother was afraid of fire.

I asked about the presents they received from Father Christmas (that is what she called Santa Claus). The children would hang up a real stocking (not like the fancy ones we see today) and in it they would receive a few hard candy and oranges. It may seem strange today, but oranges were a rarity in those days. My grandmother said she would eat hers right away as it was such a treat. She also said she might get a small china ornament in her stocking. This was never to be played with. Her mother would put it upon a shelf and it was not to be touched.

As far as gifts went there would be homemade socks, mittens and scarves. A few times there may be a sleigh made by her father, and that was to be shared by all the children. As far as toys, they were nonexistent in the family. From a young age all were expected to do chores, and simple toys were few and far between.

I asked her if she ever got a doll or teddy bear to play with. She said never. And how she longed to have either one! The store owner's daughter had gotten a doll and a teddy bear one Christmas, and my grandmother had wished she had gotten something so pretty to play with. No such thing as childhood toys in her family. And with such a large family she could not even find enough rags to make herself a rag doll. My heart broke when she told me this story.

So, the coming Christmas I would rectify this!

Christmas Day came and of course I went to visit her. She was very happy it was Christmas and opened the presents I gave to her. I don't recall what they were except for the last one. It was a lovely wrapped box with pretty paper and a large bow. She said, "What is this?" I said, "It is a special gift just for you."

Well, she opened the gift and there were tears in her eyes.

From the box she took out the most beautiful teddy bear she had ever seen. From the look on her face I could tell she was thinking back to her childhood. With tears in my eyes, I said, "At last you have your very own teddy bear to love."

And love it she did. She said she had never had anything so beautiful in her life and would cherish it forever. From that day on, her teddy bear held a special place in her heart. It sat lovingly on her bed for the rest of her life. When she died at the age of 91 and went to meet her heavenly Father, her teddy bear went with her. Together forever!

Christmas Eve, 1954

Barclay Neville

I grew up in Whitney Pier, on the corner of Victoria Road and East Broadway. My father, affectionately known in the community as Johnny Bow Tie, was a gentle giant of a man. Due to his stature, neckties were often too short so he would wear bow ties, hence the nickname.

He was also known for his willingness to help others, volunteer work, and sense of community. Christmas Eve 1954 was one such occasion that I had the privilege of joining him while he volunteered to help deliver groceries for the nearby store. I was ten years old.

When we finished delivering the groceries, my father asked me if there was anything that I wanted for my helping out. I gave it some thought and decided that I would like to get Christmas gifts for my brothers and sisters. We went back to the store where we had been helping deliver the groceries. After much consideration I decided that I would like to get each of them a bag of animal crackers. At a cost of ten cents a bag I purchased my gifts for my siblings.

I remember that day as vividly as if it was yesterday. It was my first experience purchasing Christmas gifts for others and started the tradition of gift-giving for me which I have continued throughout my life. The day was filled with the spirit of Christmas, acts of generosity, kindness, charity and family.

A Christmas Memory

Bernadette MacNeil

Christmas Day has long been my favourite time of the year, and the weeks leading up to that day are most magical. My head and heart become filled with romantic dreams of all that Christmas will be. The passion and determination to realize that special dream of magic, I learned from Christie, my dear mother. She was driven to provide me and my siblings with a perfect Christmas, complete with a warm spotless home filled with glittering lights and flickering candles. Now I want to follow in her footsteps for my family.

Christmas of 1988, at our home in East Bay, was to be no different from any other, except that I knew it was to be the beginning of a new and adventurous tradition for my own young family. Oh, my head was filled with a vision for this escapade. It was to be something we would look forward to doing as a family every year; a tradition our young sons would continue as adults when with children of their own. What a delightful and heartwarming undertaking this was to be.

On an early December morning we—my husband and I and our two young boys—set out on a blissful day to establish the family's first Christmas tree hunt. The fields were laden with a thick blanket of the clean, white, heavy stuff. What was to make this even more memorable, was that our walk through the fields and woods across from our home was to include Christmas music.

In the days without smart phones, the only way to be accompanied by the delightful sounds of Bing Crosby, Dean Martin, and Judy Garland, was to take along our ghetto blaster! Brilliant! My husband, always being one to oblige his wife's every wish, voiced no opposition. With our two toddlers bundled in layers of snow pants and heavy boots, our sled to transport our youngest because walking was not an option, our older toddler of two years, my husband carrying the very large music box on his shoulder along with the saw and the axe, we ventured out. The bright blue sky and glorious sunshine made the day that much more blissful. As we tramped through the deep snow, it was becoming obvious to me that my husband was labouring a bit with his load. Still, it was very manageable. "It's okay, dear," he explained. And soldiered on.

We came upon the most perfect tree. It took more time than I thought it would, but it was worth it. It was beautiful. Cutting it down wasn't as easy as I thought it would be. Meanwhile, our boys were getting a bit cranky as nap time was compromised in our creation of this loving memory for my family.

At last, the tree was cut down and all was well. It was time to start the journey back home. It was cumbersome to drag the tree, the music box, the axe, and the saw. The sled was now without child. Our youngest son was in no mood to play a part in the building of this memory. So, he had decided he would walk, like his older brother. Following a less than a brisk struggle through the deep snow almost reaching his bottom he surrendered, not to get in the sled, but instead, to be carried. This did however, free the sled to carry the excess baggage—the tree, the axe, the saw, and the music box. We had given up on the music anyway as the tunes were being drowned out by the whining from our boys, now anxious to have lunch. To add, a chill had set in and the wind was beginning to blow the snow around.

Seemingly, the snow was much deeper coming back than going in, but we finally arrived home. We stood our beautiful tree in a corner to dry out for the night. Tomorrow's day of decorating would be another opportunity to build that precious memory; perhaps one that we could enjoy more so than the laborious tree search.

That evening, my brother and his wife dropped by our house. Upon their departure, I opened our front door to wave goodbye. I could see that a storm was brewing. Through the night, my husband, having felt a very cold draft, got up only to discover that our front door was ajar. Sadly, I neglected to shut it tight and now a huge snowdrift covered the entrance way. But the snow was not the only invasion from the outside that night.

The next morning, our older son was overly intrigued with our beautiful Christmas tree. Still not decorated. He gleefully kept calling out to a "puddy cat." We did not have a cat. To our surprise, and our dismay, we found a very cunning and quick moving white weasel, nestled comfortably in our tree. Our decorating plan was quickly stolen by the battle to excommunicate the beady-eyed weasel from our home. "It's okay, dear. I'll get the bloody critter," my husband exclaimed. He was successful.

Peace finally came back upon our home by nightfall. With the weasel out, the boys fast asleep, the tree took back its rightful honour as a glorious and perfect Christmas tree. The time had come for a much-deserved night of rest. Decorating would be delayed until morning. We snuggled by a beautiful wood-burning fire. All was so right. All was so peaceful, except for the continuous sound of falling needles.

The tree did get decorated. It looked beautiful for all of five days. By Boxing Day, not one needle was left on our precious tree. It was stripped of its dignity, its luster, its beauty as it stood naked and surrounded by a puddle of needles at its base. I suppose our mistake was one that could be made by many. A black spruce tree is usually perfectly shaped but is a tree to be left standing in the woods, not in a home sharing a room with a wood stove.

Although denied a warm blissful memory from the tree plight of 1988, we were left with a memory none the less! A memory that reminds me of great intentions; of a husband that went along with my daydream without one complaint; of a lesson to shut the door tightly; of a lesson in horticulture; and a belief that Christmas is still the most magical time of the year!

Alexander Graham Bell's Man in the Air— Christmas Day, 1905

from a letter from Mabel Bell

First, I must ask you and Hattie's congratulations on Mr. Bell's final triumph—Lucien's exploit when he hung suspended above ground simply sufficed to show what the *Frost King* kite could do, and was as much as could have been accomplished without previous preparation. It was perfectly satisfactory to Mr. Bell at the time and we would very likely have gone home before but that Mr. Cunningham, the photographer, had chosen just that time to lock himself in the darkroom and develop some rather worthless pictures of Susie and Jack, and there was no other camera available, so the event passed unrecorded pictorially.

While a strong wind was not required—in fact I was not aware at the time that there was any—more wind was necessary, and day succeeded day and, although the lake was not always like glass, the few intermissions generally occurred at night or were too short to avail.

Finally on Christmas Day a breeze came playing hide and seek and got caught sufficiently long to allow His Majesty to ascend in all his stately dignity and hover serenely above the hilltop, but not long enough to admit of Lucien's ascending the rope ladder it had carried above when the men had pulled it down to be within his reach. You see, the kite went up itself about 300 metres (980 feet), carrying the rope ladder which commenced about 30 feet (10 metres) below and hung down 14 feet (5 metres); and in order to enable Lucien to reach the lowest rung it had to be pulled down. But before the men could get it down the wind gave out and the *Frost King* came down of his own accord and ended all experiments for the day. Douglas got good photographs in spite of the biting cold, but of course there was no spectacular aeronaut to snap shot.

The boys got discouraged and left next morning to our great regret, but we hung on desperately. More days of waiting followed; then Mr. Bell got more and more desperate and took to getting up early, and this morning just as we were finally giving up and going South he was rewarded. The wind was not a good one, in fact he says it was the worst possible, and Ferguson at the laboratory and Davidson at the Point said no use trying, but he went—a forlorn hope as again the lab was deserted except for Ferguson.

There being no lightweight men I offered my 115 pounds and Mr. Bell would have accepted but, of course, there were any number of last things to do, with no one to help, so I remained. Just as the trunks descended the stairs Mr. Bell burst into the office (formerly Daisy's room) waving the Kodak. "Develop, develop," he cried. "We've got him, and if the photos don't come out I'm not going today!" And he hustled me off downstairs to the darkroom.

Of course I had ordered it tidied up that very morning and

we lost precious time and nerve finding the developing powder but finally succeeded. Davidson mixed mine all right and I went ahead slowly and calmly in spite of Mr. Bell popping in and out the door, jumping about like a boy, and his three pictures came out beautifully, but only showed Neil MacDermid just clear of the ground. However, that was enough, and there was rejoicing and the trunks started and I went off to finish.

Meanwhile, Davidson went on with his photographs which were to show Neil in all the splendor of his 30 feet of elevation. Alas and alas, in the excitement he got hold of the wrong developer (the slow one, I believe) and when I came back I found him almost literally tearing his hair and very certainly slapping his thigh and shaking himself in high disgust and indignation in having spoiled his beauties. If only . . . I had been there we might have helped him save something, for the developer is perfectly good only he did not know it, and in despair had put his film in the hypo.

I wanted Mr. Bell to wait another day and try again as the wind still held . . . but he refused! Said those he had were sufficient. I have since found out he was too nervous to stand the strain again for he said, "You've no idea how high up he was. You don't know how high 30 feet is, it's more than twice the height of the telegraph poles, and if the rope had broken or anything on the kite had given away and Neil had fallen he would have been killed or seriously injured."

Mr. Bell hadn't meant him to go quite so high apparently, anyway he was thankful the ascent and descent had been accomplished safely without hitch or trouble anywhere, and he'd no mind to risk fortune again.

Now, as for the facts. The *Frost King* is a comparatively small and light kite. The figures as given in the newspaper account Mr. Bell sent you are fairly correct, and on this occasion it supported in the air, 30 feet from the ground, Neil weighing 165 lbs., and ropes and rope ladder bringing the total weight carried outside its own [to] 226 lbs. And this in a wind of no great strength, just a fair sailing breeze coming from the worst kite quarter so poor that Ferguson telephoned Mr. Bell that there was no use in coming down to try it . . . .

Mr. Bell is so happy and so excited underneath a very quiet demeanor—it means so terribly much to him . . . . We've just lived for this moment. Day after day we've gone to the window and turned away in despair and everyone and everything has been waiting for it. We've just existed while waiting. Susie's wedding and the boys' visit just relieved the tension a bit, but it's been awful and I'm glad we are still alive and kicking.

In later years Neil MacDermid would tell people, "I made the first flight." His kite ascension occurred four years before the first aircraft flight in Canada, the flight of the Silver Dart *in 1911.*

Silver Blades

Kinnon Quinn

Many years ago before the inception of internet and social media, children would be seen playing outside in winter months when not attending school. Sledding on snow-crusted hills, building snow forts for protection against assailing snowballs—and skating, my favourite winter activity.

It was the winter in the year 1955 when first I slipped my feet into a pair of ice skates at the age of nine. They were not pretty white figure skates but hockey skates handed down from my older brother or possibly a male cousin. Being of small stature and having tiny feet, it was necessary to stuff them with pages torn from Simpson's and Eaton's catalogues or discarded newspapers.

Wearing these cumbersome skates, I learned to stand, trip and fall on the frozen ponds in our neighbourhood. Growing up in the infamous Gannon Road area of North Sydney, the Lily Lake was easily accessible on a worn path through the woods. With cold hands and feet I would sit on a dead tree stump and lace these clunky wonderful skates as tightly as possible. After many attempts, multiple tumbles and scraped knees, I was able to some degree to master the art of skating, and each Christmas I wished to find a new pair of skates under the tree. While I waited for my wish to come true, I honed my skills using whatever hand-me-downs came my way.

I marveled at my sister, three years my senior, with a mixture of envy and admiration as she glided effortlessly on her racing skates which I so desired.

On Christmas morning in my fourteenth year my wish finally came true when beneath the tree lay a pair of racing skates with my name attached. My heart swelled. They were black leather sturdy ankle boots with long track silver blades, and best of all, no other feet had worn them; they were store-bought new. I picked them up, smelled the new leather and ran my fingers along the cold blades. I was beyond happy. When the Christmas morning rituals ended off, I hurried to Lily Lake to christen my new skates. And after a few trips over the long track blades I was confidently gliding along with ease on a crystal sheet of ice with a song in my heart and a brisk wind in my face.

Skating along with the music at the old Northside Forum will forever be one of my fondest memories. Saturday mornings I clowned with my friends and on Tuesday evenings I adopted a certain sophistication while attending adult sessions. Fortunately my dear uncle ran the forum canteen, and through his kindness I skated free of charge by working during intermissions. As I write this story, I wonder if my uncle realized the enormity of his gift to me, the young girl who so loved to skate.

In my late teens I crossed the Canso Causeway and left my

Cape Breton home in search of employment, like so many others before and after me. My racing skates came with me wherever I roamed. They were my connection to home.

Future years brought marriage and two beautiful daughters who kept their Mom busy. It was then I switched to using figure skates, a safer choice for helping little ones learn the fine art of skating. My racing skates were stored for many years in the attic of our home.

With the natural progression of time and life, our daughters grew into women, married and taught their own children to skate while Mom and Dad grew older.

Then one day a "sale pending" sign graced the property of the old family home. It was time to purge the attic. When I opened the box in which my racing skates were stored I paused, held them in my hands, examined the scars they wore from many years of use, and ran my fingers along the now dull and rusted blades. A flood of memories hastened me back to Lily Lake, to the scrape of shiny silver blades on crystal ice, to a song in my heart and a brisk wind in my face.

I smiled!

Christmas Imps

Norma Jean MacPhee

The front door closes as Mom and Dad rush out to Midnight Mass.

"Be good. We'll be home soon." Their instructions echo in their daughters' excited heads.

Two brunettes and one blonde sit in the living room admiring the Christmas tree, considering how to amuse themselves before their parents return. The house sparkles as Mom finished all touch-ups that afternoon. Cinnamonny Christmas candles and the flickering wood stove carry a warm tingling smell throughout the house. The counters beam with Eagle brand squares, jars of ginger snaps and bits and bolts, platters of fruit cake and short-breads. The morning's turkey was chillin' out in the sink.

The Christmas Eve gift opening at Nanny's unleashed the desire to tear open more mysterious treasures. Keeping with tradition in their own house, once Mom and Dad get home from Mass, they can each open one more gift. Then, with magic and love, heavy steps and tired murmurings will select pieces of furniture and leave them laden with colourful packages of all sizes. Bulging plaid Christmas socks crocheted by Nanny years earlier identify who owns each pile for the sleepy girls. But that would be later. Tomorrow morning.

For now the girls sit shaking and sniffing the gifts already piled under the tree, trying to decide which one to open first. Rosanne looks at her potentials each in careful turn. A little shake and feel, but definitely no prying of tape.

"Jo, that's cheating," she chides, as the blonde curiously leans her head down to the corner and peers beneath the puckered tape.

"I can't see anything anyway," she answers as her wide, round blue eyes feign innocence.

"Let's play something," Rosanne suggests by way of distraction.

Aunt Rita had delivered her annual board game gift that afternoon. *Personal Preference* looked a little easier than the *Trivial Pursuit* of last year. With the dining room table all ready, the ladies take up shop in the kitchen. Laughs erupt as they rediscover each other's likes and dislikes.

But excitement and wonder still fester in the blonde's head. Jolane wanders toward the bathroom and continues to meander down the forbidden hall leading to Mom and Dad's room. She knows Christmas Eve onward, the area beyond the hall mirror is out of bounds, but she presses on.

"I don't want to know," comes from Rosanne's lips, while Norma Jean sits on the fence for a bit. Then, curiosity tugs her tail down the hall too. Like having an angel and devil on her shoulders, she's torn between wanting to know but still not really wanting to know. She silences the angel and joins Jo.

Looking around, they ponder where to start. The closet is so close, so easy; but too much, too soon. Sliding her hand under the mattress, Jolane hits something hard. With the help of her accomplice, they hoist the top mattress to discover blue, green and red crazy carpets. Yehaw—those babies will fly down Harold Street. When the mattress flumps back, the closet still looms.

"Guys, let's play cards," comes the voice of reason near the hallway bathroom.

Temptation wins over reason and the closet draws closer. They inch across the carpet. Slowly, deliberately. Doorknob turns. Angel. Devil. Angel. The door creaks open.

But Santa is smarter than she/he looks. Dress shirts, sweaters and blouses and slacks smile back at the meddling imps. Meanwhile, their gifts languish in Nanny's sewing room.

Pleased to have searched, with their wondering thirst quenched, they trot back down the hall to the living room. Anticipation still pumps in the blood.

Nibbling on nuts and bolts and the surviving chocolate balls, the three girls wait for their parents' return.

Chewing and mumbling. Haveagh pfatinish. Not much longer now.

The Post Office Christmas

Duncan MacEachern

The year was 1948 or 1949. Christmas was a busy time at our home. We had a store and also the post office in our house. It served all the Murray, Oregon and Meadow Roads, along with the North River and Tarbot areas. The mail driver was a very large man, close to three hundred pounds, and he drove a very small car. There was a lot of mail, packages from the USA, Simpson Sears and Eaton's mail order stores, and lots of cards and letters.

This Christmas Eve day was very snowy and windy. The mail driver arrived around 9:30 in the morning to pick up the mail. Because of the bad weather, he had his horse and a large sleigh with a box on board to hold the bags.

People started gathering at our house around dark, which was about 4:30 p.m. The mail was always late on snowy days.

It being Christmas Eve, me and my younger brother would want to be in bed before Santa came. So by 5:00 p.m. we were all ready for bed. But with all the people in and out, there was a lot of noise and commotion and we couldn't get to sleep. There was a lot of singing and shouting, and we didn't think Santa would come with all the noise.

Finally we heard someone say, "He's coming!" and to us it could have been the mailman or Santa, and we were afraid Santa wouldn't stop if there were people up and about. Finally we heard the sleigh bells and we peeked out the window. It was fairly bright because the light from the Aladdin's lamps shining through the store windows was fairly bright. We could see the shadow of a large man carrying a large bag. We still weren't sure who it was, but we were very excited thinking it might be Santa and we had better try to get to sleep.

Before I slept, my sister brought me a Christmas card from a friend in Baddeck with a five-dollar bill inside. Everyone was excited then.

We must have fallen asleep—because when we went downstairs in the morning, we saw that Santa HAD been there, and left lots of toys and fruit and candy for everyone!

Six Potatoes

Anne Camus

This happened roughly forty years ago in the '80s, when I lived in St. Catharines, Ontario, a city near Niagara Falls, with a population of 130,000 people.

I worked as a cleaning lady. Of my customers, I worked for this one couple—a United Church minister and his wife, a school teacher. Very nice and religious people.

Mrs. Hershey taught in jails to try and educate prisoners to have a better life, once they got their liberty again. Also she taught social skills to disabled people.

This one man "Peter," about sixty-five or seventy years old, was one of her students. He'd been diagnosed as being deaf mute and mentally challenged—referred to as "retarded" in those days.

He'd been abused by his parents as a child. He was not to be seen. They were ashamed of his condition. As he got older he was put in care in this institution run by the government. One day a heavy object was dropped and he jumped. Upon many tests, it was discovered he could hear. Mrs. Hershey became his caregiver, teaching him social skills and how to talk. He'd go to the Hersheys and worked for them doing odd jobs. He was being paid minimum wages, so it wouldn't affect his disability pension. The Hersheys were very good to him, spending the summer months at their cottages in northern Ontario. He'd plant a beautiful vegetable garden every year, did yard work and other light jobs. Eventually he moved into his own apartment and took care of himself. A lady helped with shopping and household chores.

Christmas was upon us. He didn't live very far from my family. Five or so miles. This one Saturday, I picked him up to go to the Hersheys, as I was going there myself. I brought two homemade apple pies for the Hersheys and one for Peter as Christmas gifts.

Ready to leave, the Hersheys gave us each a Christmas card with money, a fruit cake for me and some Christmas cookies for Peter.

A few days later was Christmas Eve. Wet snow was falling on a very chilly night. We were getting ready to go to the Midnight Mass. It was 10:45 p.m. and this knock came on the door. What a surprise to see Peter with his grey mustache full of ice and runny nose. His bicycle by the house, hauling a 3-wheel cart behind. I invited him to come in for a coffee to get warmed up. He was carrying a brown paper bag, tied with a red ribbon. He said, "This is for you," and wanted me to open it.

The best Christmas gift I ever received: six medium-sized potatoes. Of course tears rolled down my cheeks while our two children rolled their eyes in disbelief. To me this is what Christmas is all about: "True Love."

Merry Christmas, and enjoy your potatoes.

The Blessing of the Beggar

Ludger D'Amour

On Christmas Eve 1956, we were living in St. Bonaventure parish in Ottawa. We had four children. There were two Christmas Masses, one at midnight and another in the morning at 10 o'clock.

My wife Gertrude would stay at home with the children in the evening so that I could attend Midnight Mass. In the morning, she would go to mass with the two older girls, Hélène, six and Cécile, four, while I stayed with the younger ones, Jean-Marie, three and Martine, fifteen months.

Our Christmas celebration at 1400 Raven Street included a Christmas story in front of the fireplace, a few forty-five rpm records of Christmas music and a polka. The entertainment and music were my share of the parental education.

I had set up the Christmas tree with a few decorations from past years and a few splats of plaster of Paris to imitate snow. We had placed a gift for each one under the tree, as well as individual Christmas cards with a personal love message for each one.

As we lived a short distance from the church, I set out on foot to go to Midnight Mass. I enjoyed the weather and marvelled at the beautiful decorations of the richer homes along the way.

When I got close to the church, I was approached by a young man with a beard who asked me to help him and his family have a decent Christmas.

I had a five-dollar bill in my pocket, my Christmas collection money. On the spur of the moment, without questioning or judging the gentleman beggar, I handed him the five dollars.

He was very polite, wishing me a Merry Christmas and added so sincerely, "God will bless you."

I had a one dollar bill left for church collection and we had all we needed at the house to celebrate.

Next morning, the early to bed were early to rise and even before breakfast, the wrappings were stripped off and everyone enjoyed their gifts and their messages of love. I thought of the simple tranquility of my young family, enjoying the warm atmosphere of home where love was shared by everyone and no one had a worry in the world.

Was this the blessing offered by the gentleman beggar the night before? I assumed it was.

Life continued with the occasional worry about health and periods of financial insecurity, but we managed to survive and we moved to Montreal two years later.

Ten years after that, the children were all in school and the company I worked for closed down its construction department.

I was out of work. I tried selling equipment, but it didn't pay enough to support my growing family.

I longed to start a business of my own. I had an idea that I could make money manufacturing steel shelving for grocery stores. I had no experience in sheet metal work and the equipment to do the job was much more than I could afford. I tried to borrow money from two banks and was turned down. With nowhere to turn, I went to a high interest finance company to borrow the required capital. With my balance sheet and my lack of experience, I knew that even there, my chances of getting a Cape Breton's Christmas loan were slim. I wanted $7000 to be repaid over three years.

Next day I got the answer by phone; my loan was granted.

The first three years were not easy, but my business survived. When I went to make the last payment on my loan, I asked the manager what made him decide to loan me the money in the first place, I had so little collateral.

He would not tell me, he just said, "Sometimes small things can make a big difference."

My business developed into a successful venture and supported my family very well. For many years, I forgot about that Christmas Eve in Ottawa, the blessing of the gentleman beggar and my unexpected loan.

Last week, more than 45 years after the fact, I had a dream of those years of struggle and hardship. In my dream, I met two men, neither one had a beard. They came smiling to me and one told me his friend knew me from a long time ago when he was a beggar on a certain Christmas Eve in Ottawa. He said his friend had gotten a job as manager in a finance company and he had recognized me when I applied for the loan.

Now I wonder, was this a dream or was it my subconscious working out a mystery that had stayed with me for so many years?

It would explain why I was granted a loan and it would explain the manager's comment, "Sometimes small things can make a big difference."

It would also explain the blessings of the poor . . . but maybe blessings need no explanation.

Faceplant

Tom Ross

You're familiar, perhaps, with the type of contest that radio stations run at Christmas time—the "sounds of Christmas" contest. A caller phones in and tries to identify various recorded sounds which are emblematic of Christmas. The hissing sound of a turkey in the oven, the scraping sound of clearing a windshield of ice and snow, the rustling of wrapping paper. All pretty commonplace.

But what is that mysterious splatting, thudding sound followed by a low groan? That is the sound of long-dry alcoholics falling off the wagon. That is the sound of nose meeting pavement, heard at different times and places throughout the city during December. If the owner of the nose has been lucky, there is a cushioning of snow to buffer the fall and minimize the injuries. Ralph usually didn't have that kind of luck.

Ralph had been "dry" for a long stretch this time. Seven years. The same length of time Marley had been dead before re-appearing to Scrooge. Ralph was beginning to feel that he may be revisited by his own ghosts of Christmas Past this year. It was just a feeling, indefinable, but he knew these feelings, he knew how they played out. He knew it might be time to call Ed, his sponsor in A.A., and maybe make "a searching and fearless moral inventory of himself" as Step 4 suggested. This might buy him some time, help him get past December. It's amazing how terms like "get past," "get through," and "survive" December have become part of the lexicon surrounding the Holidays. It's as though Christmas is an endurance event or a plague. But if you are an alcoholic, if you're jonesing for a drink, Christmas may feel like both those things.

Ralph could feel his personal barometer rising. Nothing specific, a bit of this and a bit of that, but he could feel himself being drawn inexorably towards "the drink." It might be a big thing, or something quite inconsequential and trivial, but inevitably something would occur that lit up those parts of Ralph's brain that would open the gates and wash it in a wave of ethanol.

People liked Ralph, and Ralph liked people. He was avuncular, overweight, balding, fiftyish. He was harmless, happy, undemanding, and got along with everyone, all the attributes needed for success in his job as an advertising salesperson for the

Langdon Standard. Been with the paper for years, and had climbed the ladder about as high as he was going to go. He didn't want to be sales manager or V.P., and no one was going to offer him those positions. He didn't pose a threat to anyone's job, and was content with his own. Always with a good story gleaned from one of his associates on his city beat.

It depends how broad your definition of an "alcoholic" is, if you would even consider Ralph an alcoholic. Seven years clean and sober—if it were cancer you'd be called a "survivor" not a cancer patient. But nobody calls alcoholics survivors, as if they have come out the other side of something horrible. They continue with their status as alcoholics even if they, like Ralph, haven't indulged in years. Perhaps that's why in Spanish there are two forms of the verb "to be." ESTAR which is used to describe something impermanent like happiness or being drunk, and then there is SER which describes something immutable, an inherent part of your being, like being an alcoholic. Thus, "yo soy Ralph, soy un alcoholico"—I am Ralph, I am an alcoholic.

Ralph didn't have some of the classic behaviours attendant to the condition. He didn't hide a bottle in his desk, he'd never missed work with a hangover, he didn't abuse Marion or take her grocery money. But he did share with his fellow pursuers of this particular poison a deep-seated, all-encompassing need that only a bottle could satisfy. Yes, Ralph was an alcoholic no matter what your definition.

Christmas is a busy time for an ad salesman. A good December can really pull your numbers up for the year, stand you in good stead for a decent bonus. The young Turks in the sales department were really after it, making calls, filling their appointment books. Ralph had his regular accounts, contacts he'd had for years. He had seen enough Christmases to know how it went, but the feeling in the office was a bit contagious, like a cold. You couldn't be immune to it, and would find yourself pressing a little harder to garner a new client or two. Maybe it was this insidious pressure that finally caused Ralph to take that fatal first drink. Perhaps it was because it was late on a Friday afternoon in mid-December, the end of the work week during the height of the festive season. Maybe it was because he was wearing Argyll socks that day, who knows? But something conspired within Ralph so that when he had concluded his last appointment at Johnson's Accounting Services, and Al Johnson suggested he have a beer with him, Ralph had about as much power to decline the invitation as the ocean's tide to resist the influence of the full moon.

Now, when you're an alcoholic and you haven't been "practicing" for a while, let alone seven years, your liver enzymes are out of shape and don't metabolize booze as efficiently. In Ralph's case, they were downright lethargic. That first beer hit him like a meteor. Parts of his brain, long quiescent, were lighting up like a mall Christmas tree. All the worries of the season evaporated, he immediately felt as if he had returned home after a long sojourn in a foreign land. There was no easing into it for Ralph, he was full-bore "on," the devil take the hindmost.

There are likely as many euphemisms to describe being drunk as the natives of the North use to describe snow. A clever comic once recited twenty-six terms to describe Ralph's present condition, each word beginning with a different letter of the alphabet. Ralph's state encompassed all those terms. He was on a tear and the closing hour of the pub was not going to mark the end of Ralph's evening. Out on the street in front of the pub, a light snow had begun to fall, which added considerably to the navigational problems Ralph was experiencing. But he needed to find another place open at this hour. Even in this state, he knew he didn't have anything to drink at home. He wandered a block or two through the downtown core until he heard the sound of music coming out of a dimly lit building. He could see people inside sitting at candlelit tables. It looked warm and inviting as the snow clung to his coat.

The front door was locked but Ralph could hear a side entrance open as a couple came out. He careened down the alley and gave the door a heave. It opened, admitting Ralph and a gust of snow into a coffee house where the sounds of "Blowin' in the Wind" were being played acoustically by a couple seated on a small stage. Ralph surveyed the scene—young folks lounging on old sofas, a few scattered tables, candles everywhere, and a huge, batik wall-hanging at the rear. A natural tree twinkled in the corner. It seemed a pretty unlikely place to get a beer. It was 1:30 a.m. and snowing. Ralph weighed his options, with as much as he had left for critical faculties, and made the decision to sit down. He lurched towards a table with a vacant chair. A beautiful young woman approached him and, wishing him a Merry Christmas, asked him what he wanted. "I'll have a Keith's," Ralph replied. "Sorry, sir, this is a coffee house, we don't serve alcohol," she told him.

This wasn't what Ralph hoped to hear. Again, he needed to make a decision. "Gimme a coffee, then," he slurred. When she returned with the coffee, Ralph sat quietly sipping it and listening to the music. None of the young people took any notice of him, engaged as they were in their own conversations and coffee. Ralph tapped his foot as he listened, while the musicians, who were actually quite good, strummed "Michael Row the Boat Ashore." Ralph was still wearing his tie, although it was askew, and his order book was crammed into the pocket of his overcoat. He hadn't eaten since lunch, except for a few snacks at the bar. Not much to absorb a night's drinking.

Now there are very few instances which constitute a real loss of "dignity," although there are lots of instances in which the word is used, or misused, perhaps more so around the Christmas season. Well-meaning types speak of giving "dignity" to a needy family by delivering a turkey hamper and some gifts to them. People speak, often, of losing their "dignity" when they're in hospital and require assistance toileting. However, "dignity" is something that someone can neither bestow upon or take away from an individual. It is an inherent part of our condition as humans, immune to the doings of others. But Ralph was about to test the limits of that theory.

The couple up front were winding down, thanking everyone, and wishing them the best of the season. They launched into a jazzy intro which eventually worked itself into "Have Yourself a Merry Little Christmas." It was a quiet, almost spiritual moment in a warm, darkened room in a snowy, sleeping city. This third decision that Ralph would make since entering the coffee house did not require the executive function of his addled brain. No, it was a purely instinctive, visceral response, from spinal cord to Ralph's feet, with no ascension of nerve impulses to his cerebral cortex.

In a second he was on his feet, moving with slow grace around the small, open area in front of the musicians. Arms outstretched, eyes closed, a rapturous look on his face, his overcoat swinging with his movements as he nimbly danced about. It's a bit of a physical oxymoron how drunks can be so light on their feet, but Ralph was almost balletic in his movements. He glided through the space keeping perfect time with the rhythm and not saying a word, as if he had been lifted by the music to a different time and place.

The whole scenario seemed to, somehow, fit the occasion—Christmas, cold outside, a time of tolerance and understanding, a quiet moment late on a dark night. No one shouted at Ralph to sit down, the couple playing guitars supported his pirouettes and flourishes. When the music stopped there was a hush in the room for a few seconds, then a ripple of applause built throughout the audience. Ralph opened his eyes and looked about bewildered. Then he made an elaborate bow. He hadn't landed on his nose.

My Dolls

Reyonalda MacDonald

When I was a little child, four or five, my mother always took turns taking my sister Mary and I into the "big city" of Sydney. This was my special turn to go, so off we went. It must have been near Christmas, because as we walked down Charlotte Street, there was Santa Claus. My mother asked me if I would stepdance for Santa and I would get a Shirley Temple doll for Christmas. I didn't mind as my brother John and I always stepdanced for everyone who came to the house to visit us. So needless to say, I stepdanced for Santa and I got my Shirley Temple doll for Christmas.

I played with that doll forever, but while playing with her, I left her on a mat on the kitchen floor. In the meantime, my father came from outside with his rubber boots on, holding a load of wood on his arm, obstructing his view of the floor. He stepped on my doll, crushing her face, which was made of porcelain, breaking her, never to be fixed.

I learned an expensive lesson that day, to never leave your toys on the floor. Needless to say, we couldn't afford to have the beloved doll replaced.

Until my aunt Annie MacKinnon presented me with another doll for my birthday in March. It wasn't a Shirley Temple doll but I loved her and took her everywhere I went.

One day in the summer, we children—five of us—were playing on our gate at the end of the road, swinging on it, which we enjoyed very much.

I had taken my doll down to the road for safekeeping. While

I played on the gate. I carefully laid her on the bank outside the gate to keep her safe.

In the meantime, my father who owned a little store, kept a watch on his children. My mother had died. He yelled from the store for us to fly home and stop playing on the gate, so near the main road. Needless to say, when we heard my father yell, we immediately left the gate and ran to the house.

From our house, I sadly watched two girls who were walking down the main road. They discovered my doll and walked off with her. There was nothing I could do about it, but go without that precious doll.

I don't recall getting another doll until we were grown adults. My sister Theresa bought me a Shirley Temple doll which I still treasure.

Feasted and Immovable

Taiya Barss

Eating is one of the most satisfying and pleasurable necessities of life, although only truly appreciated when hungry.

I invite people to dinner, but never offer them canapés or appetizers. Why should I slave over a hot stove preparing breaded, sautéed chicken breast sprinkled with candied kumquat peel, potatoes sliced thin as paper, layered with melted butter and baked golden, tiny peas, barely cooked and sprinkled with mint, only to have guests called to the table, groaning as they rise up with bellies already filled with crackers, cheese and smoked oysters?

I require hunger.

Even a lowly hamburger, perhaps with a bit of blue cheese added, pickled red onions, and a thick slice of ripe tomato, can reach the same plane as, say, lobster Newburg, if it is napped and sauced with enough gnawing hunger.

But Christmas arrives and buries any pangs but pangs of guilt in rolls of toffee, chocolates, turkey and stuffing, potatoes and gravy. Fruitcake, that annual brown brick, heavy with raisins and currants, pecans, tart apricots and chewy figs, with just enough dark, sticky batter to hold it all together. It seems to grow bigger during Christmas week, despite chipping away at it, and there is still a fat chunk left after Christmas. It stares at me until I succumb. When I have crammed all of it down, I no longer have to worry about the calories sitting there, waiting for me.

Chocolate truffles. I couldn't eat them even when I was the one who made them, before passing the chore on to my son. Butter and chocolate, melted together, cooled, then rolled into balls and coated with cocoa. Keep them chilled. Left on their own, at room temperature, they turn into small brown puddles of sweet fat.

This season, there is so much food, just sitting out, within reach, beckoning. Figs like soft leather, their seeds crunching . . . nuts to crack, then pick out the sweet meat . . . peanut brittle, so easy to make, I can eat it all, and just whip up another batch. A bag of dollar store peanuts, lots of sugar, a microwave, and Voila!

Indulging, binging, filled, stuffed, sated, feasted and fattened.

Hunger, where is thy pang?

Come, meager January, lean and mean, come quickly, please save me!

Cherishing the Christmas Cherries

Beverly Romeo-Bechler

You can imagine a little girl about seven from Sydney Mines.

To this day I look for the cherry chocolate to relive those past moments.

After Christmas Morning Mass, with the Barra MacNeils playing as we go, we'd dash home for the big turkey dinner with all the trimmings.

Times were tough growing up. We never had a roast or prime cuts of meat. A can of corned beef made into gravy and served over mashed potatoes would feed a family of eight. But at Christmas the turkey dinner was on the table.

Dinners like that happened once (at most, twice) a year, and if you knew us, you would know that we loved Christmas dinner almost as much as the toys.

Together with Mom and Dad, us kids—Dale, Anne, John, Donna, Beverly, and Debbie—we would eat until we were absolutely stuffed.

After dinner we'd take a run down home to Nanny Romeo's for singing and carrying on, teasing one another, and a taste of meatballs before going on to Nanny McIntyre's in the evening.

Nanny McIntyre had very little to subsist on. While our family of eight had very little to live on with a coal miner's pay, Nanny McIntyre had much less. Her dad, a coal miner, died young in a mining accident. Her mom and sister also died early, leaving Nanny to raise her little sister along with ten of her own. Nanny's husband Dada was also a coal miner and in those days shifts weren't steady, and so he took any shift he could get—until he was fifty-five when he was killed by colon cancer, leaving Nanny with children still in school and little money to go around.

But if times were tough, Nanny was tough as nails and as proud as they come. With no income and too proud to take welfare, she got along somehow until she received old age security. Coal was ten dollars a ton for widows of coal miners. As Nanny said, "Cheap coal for the widow's home was the only death benefit for coal miners." Not much, but it was enough to heat her house.

Nanny would never ask for anything, but there was an unspoken code of sharing. People just seemed to know she could use a little help and pitched in without grazing her dignity. Uncle Gordon would bring down a feed of smelt or mackerel when they were running. The boys caught rabbits for rabbit pie for after Midnight Mass. We all (twelve kids in total plus Mom, Dad, Nanny, Uncle Jackie, Aunt Phyllis and Uncle Vic) picked gallons and gallons and gallons and gallons of blueberries for Nanny's pies. "If you don't pick, you don't eat," Ma would say. So we picked and picked in the summer knowing the fruits of our labours would be right there on that table at Christmas.

We all knew she loved us, but Nanny was not one to show her emotions. And after so much loss and hardship in her life, she seldom let her guard down to let anyone close—that is, until Christmas. And maybe that is why we loved going there. At Christmastime we would target our arrival at her home for the evening time, hoping that Uncle Gordon would be playing a few tunes on the piano in the front room. I mean, just the drive to Nanny McIntyre's was filled with excitement and anticipation, and when the car stopped in her driveway the eight of us piled out. Into the porch we'd go, boots and coats flung off, trying to be the first ones to the living room. Nanny's house smelled like Christmas and rabbit pie with the biscuit crust warmed up with gravy, the sweetness of blueberry pies from the blueberries we'd picked in the summer, and of course that huge turkey.

Nanny's front room was sacred and when I say "front room" I don't mean "living room." You certainly would not live there. You went in once a year. We really weren't allowed in her front room, except on Christmas, and it was there that she kept a dish of hard candy and a dish of ribbon candy. According to Ma, we were allowed to choose just one. We got Ma's warning before we arrived! "Now remember"—finger pointing—"you are only allowed to take one and just one and if I catch you taking more, none of yays will get any . . . ." We kept each other in line, following the orders, so that we all wouldn't lose out.

There we'd be, admiring each dish of candy, weighing the pros and cons of which succulent treasure to choose. Strategizing, we'd try to look like we were being polite by letting others go first, just so that you could see if they liked their selection, so as to not waste our own choice.

While in the front room you couldn't help but feel the glow of Nanny's tree. Her Christmas trees were always enormous, big at the bottom and narrow at the top (just like a Hershey's kiss chocolate), awkward and somehow beautiful at the same time. It had to be the last one in the yard. I heard tell of the boys tying two trees together, then cutting off lower branches and tying them to the upper tree to fatten it up, because, well, that's the way Nanny liked it. And there were so many coloured lights that the glow made you feel warm.

Whatever it was, whatever the boys did to that tree, it was always big, it was always brilliant, it was love.

It was then, on Christmas, just that one time, with all her family around her in the front room, that we could see Nanny's harsh veneer soften, her heart open just a crack and her Christmas glow appear. And there she was: perched on the flat arm of the couch beside the tree, with Uncle Gordon on the piano warmed up from a drink of rum, and with twelve kids sitting on the floor or straddling the laps of the many adults—everyone singing. It was as if the tree was radiating her love, and she knew it. It was as if all the hardship, all the preparations, all the work, was for this moment.

All the love that Nanny found so hard to put into words was said that night, that year, every year, beside her tree, surrounded by a Christmas glow, surrounded by her children and grandchildren, with the piano dancing to "Christmas in Killarney" and us singing "Joy to the World" on that "Oh Holy Night"—and then it would come . . . .

This is what we had been waiting for. With a break in the music, Nanny would pull it out—the "Pot of Gold" box of candies. And while it may have felt like Christmas before this, this was *really* Christmas.

Imagine a kid not being able to have many candies in their lives. Then lo and behold—no, not the Christmas Angel; no, not Santa and eight tiny raindeer—but a whole box of "Pot of Gold." Two layers of chocolates circling the room, levitating across fingers. Being ogled over by oodles of eyes, eyes that were glancing up one row and down another, searching like a search light, little hands outstretched to examine the chunks, only to receive the scolding from Ma to stop malling and "If you touch it you take it." At which point you'd try to look disinterested as the other picker's eyes skimmed the selections. There was no way you would give away your favourite—the cherry chocolate!

And if you were lucky enough to get the cherry chocolate, you would savour that first bite, sitting on the front room floor, music playing, tree shining, Nanny glowing, love surrounding, voices raised in song with the smell of turkey, rabbit and blueberry pie engulfing the house.

But of course there were never enough cherry chocolates for everyone. Too many kids. So you would offer your second bite to another kid to see if they wanted a taste. "Everything tastes better when shared," or so Mom would say.

And if it turned out that you didn't get the Christmas cherry chocolate, you were never really disappointed. It was the anticipation and the hope that made your day, the happiness you felt for the kid that did get it, and the optimism that you carried for being the lucky one next year.

Our Christmas, 2016

Lisa MacDougall

"It was the best of times, it was the worst of times"—Charles Dickens

My mother Joan comes from a large family—seven boys and seven girls—pretty common for Cape Breton back in the day. Born in Newfoundland in 1938, she "immigrated" to New Waterford with her parents and five other siblings in 1944. Her father Allan was a coal miner and, although money was not plentiful, they grew up with lots of love. Her mother Gertie made sure they were all well fed and well clothed. Strong family values were instilled: to love and look out for each other. "Looking out for each other" would never be so evident as it was that Christmas of 2016.

Joan was married in August 1964, and had celebrated fifty-two years of wedded bliss with my dad Neil that summer of 2016. After the devastation of the Thanksgiving Floods, Mom had an appointment with a heart specialist in Halifax. Our fears were confirmed when we were advised that she would have to undergo open heart surgery and the date would be set for December 2, 2016.

Half an hour before we were set to leave for Halifax, the hospital called to reschedule, as there had been an emergency.

Our new date was booked quickly for Friday, December 16, 2016. At the time, we naively thought we would be there over the weekend while Mom was in the hospital and back home to Cape Breton at the beginning of the following week. Boy, were we wrong! No one could have predicted that her total in-facility recovery—yes, she did recover!—would be ten weeks, not the anticipated four days.

It was a given that I would accompany my parents for this life-changing medical procedure, leaving my husband Bert to deftly look after our home, our kids—Lauren, 12, and Daniel, 10—and their busy schedules.

To know me is to know I love lobster, pizza, champagne and Christmas . . . not necessarily at the same time and not necessarily in that order. But Christmas is pretty high up on my list of favourites, and so are the preparations and traditions for this beautiful and meaningful holiday.

With Mom's heart surgery date set, we tried to get as much done as possible for the upcoming holiday season, expecting that much of my time upon our return could be focused on assisting my parents as my mother recuperated post surgery.

The day of our departure to Halifax came quickly.

The drive to Halifax was a snowy one, with slippery roads and whiteout conditions. While a winter wonderland is lovely in Christmas movies, that stress-filled drive to Halifax took seven hours. Not the start we were hoping for to an already worrisome trip. We were very relieved to arrive at our Halifax hotel near the hospital, and further grateful that Mom and Dad had been upgraded to a suite for their night before the big surgery. Thus began a multitude of profound and humbling kindnesses.

Our expectation at the time was for a normal five-to-six-night stay, including the first night of our arrival with Mom pre-surgery. Little did we know, that we would actually have two weeks there, leading us to spend Christmas at the hotel while Mom remained in the hospital.

The morning of the surgery Dad and I were with Mom for an early morning start at 6:30 a.m. while she was taken for surgery prep.

During the procedure, designated family and friends of the patient are taken to the hospital's family room to wait for their loved one. On the day of Mom's surgery, there were four families there, waiting to hear news. We even had fellow "New Waterforders" with us, as the MacPherson clan had their father there for heart repair. There was also a nurse who was assigned to update the families as each patient underwent their multi-hour procedure.

The wait was long and arduous, and the people in that room talked about why they were there and who they were supporting. Three fathers—one from Halifax, one from PEI, and one from Cape Breton—and one mother—mine!

It was a day of sharing, support, and bonding. As the nurse came to report on one patient after another, we were all in it together. We braced ourselves for those hourly reports. Anticipation ran high in the family room.

While the three gentlemen went into surgery and post-op as expected, my mother and her body had other plans. She did not wake up for three days! Three, long worrisome days. As all the other parents were meeting their post-surgical milestones, mine was not. Joan, whom we affectionately called "sleeping beauty," was on her own schedule, regardless of who was waiting or what normal medical milestones were to be met.

As the other patients had their ventilation tubes removed and came through with varying degrees of alertness that day, our Joan just slept, remaining unconscious and oblivious.

The morning after Mom's surgery, we were told Mom had two seizures in the middle of the night while in ICU. Thankfully there was a nurse at the end of the bed and medication was administered immediately. We didn't know what the full implications of this would be. We just knew that her milestones came and went, and she was still not waking up.

While fearing the unknown, we also saw the best of humanity.

In our moments of despair, we were cradled in the kindness of those around us—the caring hospital physicians and staff, our fellow families who quickly became friends and confidants, and our own family and friends who brought their love and support when it was most needed.

Dad and I tried to maintain a semblance of routine. We had breakfast every morning in the hotel, then off to the hospital for the waiting game and the hope that today would be the day that we would get the good news that Joan was awake and the surgery successful.

Some of my most poignant memories are of Dad sitting at her bedside in ICU, holding her hand, for hours on end. He would also gently tap the bottom of her foot, asking her to please wake up. We watched many of the attending medical staff do the same. As my Uncle Gary once said years ago, if Neil and Joan don't make it, there is no hope for the rest of us.

It was hard not to let despair set in.

On the third day, during breakfast, the strain of the grave situation was starting to take its toll. We—me especially—were starting to worry about the "what if's" and hoped, like so many families holding vigil for their beloved family members, that a miracle would soon happen. Dad chose optimism that day, believing that things would turn around. And he was right.

On that third day, our sleeping beauty opened her eyes. Our joy quickly turned to concern when she said she felt heavy on her left side. Neurology was called right away and a CT scan was taken on her brain. It was confirmed she had two strokes that first night after surgery—thus the heaviness she felt. Thankfully, because of the ICU protocols in place and the medication administered within a minute of the seizures, the lasting and common stroke effects were averted—thankfully, no paralysis or speech impediment.

We now knew what we were dealing with, and the cardiac

staff were reassuringly competent and helpful. The next few weeks were critical to Mom's recovery, and the hospital and hotel would dominate our sheltered world.

Recovery was the focus and we were ready to do whatever was needed. So were our friends and family. We were blessed beyond measure with love and support. We had so many people step up to help us, it was humbling and beautiful.

As many families can attest, medical crisis can incur financial crisis. During our now two-week stay at the hotel, my mother's siblings chipped in and paid for the hotel room, in addition to the two nights afforded by the hospital social worker.

When it became apparent that Christmas was going to be spent at the hospital, we booked another room for my husband and children to join me for the holidays. This was the week between Christmas and New Year's. The front desk clerk had a good giggle telling me that a couple of nights had been paid for and I was to be told it was "from Santa." After some super sleuthing I found it was my dear friend and neighbour Ellen who had helped us. My beloved Newfoundland family had made arrangements with the hotel and covered a few nights as well, and my Aunt Dale had sent some money. Our family's hotel rooms were covered by the generosity of our family and friends!

It did not stop there. My cousin Tiffany and then fiancé (now husband) Mike prepared an amazing picnic for Dad and I, which we hungrily devoured in a back room off of the family room. It was a feast! Thoughtful care packages arrived, including one from my cousin Melanie with chocolates and magazines for when Mom felt up to enjoying them.

We had daily visits from friends and relatives. We had endless coffee and tea deliveries along with sandwiches and meals, sweats and treats. A place to do our laundry, dinner invitations, shoulders to cry on, and many, many hugs. My friends far and near checked in on a regular basis to see that we were okay and if I needed anything. An abundance of blessings!

We got to know the staff in the hospital cafeteria, and the hotel staff. We became close to the other "original" families of the family room, and during those first days, we shared much.

There were a couple of hours in the afternoon at the hospital held as quiet time for the patients, with no visiting. Dad would go back to the hotel during this time to read and/or nap, and I would usually go to the mall to do some—you guessed it—Christmas shopping.

While the hospital itself was decked out with "Holiday Greetings," I noticed that the family room was devoid of any such decoration.

I purchased a twelve-inch, clear, acrylic LED Christmas tree that changed colour when turned on. It was small enough not to be intrusive, but still gave a respectful nod to the holiday. Positioned in front of the window, it not only illuminated the family room with a lovely glow but also could be seen from patient ward rooms. I guess it was my way of literally providing a beacon of light in the darkness of worry. It remained the only decoration in the family room for the duration of our stay.

Christmas drew closer and arrangements needed to be made. We now knew the holidays were going to look different this year.

Although it would have been far easier and more efficient for my husband and children to come to the Halifax hotel for Christmas, the kids really wanted to wake up in their own house on Christmas morning. The planning began.

One of the cardiac families, living locally, loaned us an artificial Christmas tree and ornaments to be put up in our hotel room for the kids. Another family gave us decorations to decorate Mom's hospital room.

The hotel staff were wonderful. We were upgraded to a suite for Christmas Day night in anticipation of my children's arrival. My Dad was in charge of setting up the tree, assisted by our favourite concierge, Dylan. Dylan was a helpful, athletic college student with a caring nature. He always went above and beyond, and holds a special place in our hearts. Dylan and Dad had quite the adventure moving the tree into the elevator, then setting it up with lights and ornaments. Tiffany and Mike planned a covert mission to thoughtfully add elegant Christmas décor to the suite. I had picked up some munchies and beverages as well as some smaller gifts to be placed under the tree. Things were taking shape in my absence that Christmas Eve, and the kindnesses shown to us were ever present.

At the grocery store I was chatting with a younger sales clerk, explaining the situation that brought me to getting treats for a hotel Christmas. She asked me to hold on for a few minutes, she had something in her car she wanted me to have. She ran out on a quick break and came back to gift me a lovely glass ball ornament with white feathers in it. She had made it, and wanted me to have a reminder that angels were with me and helping with my mother's recovery. My eyes welled with tears and I hugged her, a complete stranger, to thank her for her thoughtfulness and caring. I promised I would cherish her meaningful gift and have kept true to my word.

Christmas Eve was upon us. Our friend David, originally from Sydney, living in Halifax, was heading back to Cape Breton for Christmas and was my designated driver. David picked me up at the hospital on Christmas Eve and made our trip back home a marvelous, distracting adventure by stopping at the Christmas Shop in St. Peters, where I picked up a couple of tree ornaments to commemorate this unusual, yet blessed Christmas. One was a white dove, symbolic of love and peace, and honouring my Mom's penchant for birds.

I was so excited to be reunited with my husband and kids. It had been a grueling and emotionally exhausting week. Just getting to hold everyone in my arms, savouring all those hugs, was pure bliss.

We went to my cousin's house in New Waterford for our traditional family gathering after Christmas Eve Church service—great company and great food! We stopped by our neighbours Ellen and Dave and had a nice Christmas toast with dear friends. Then off to bed so Santa could make an appearance.

We woke up the next morning, opened gifts, had breakfast, and off we went. After a visit with Bert's Mom, my beloved mother-in-law, we hit the road. Travelling on Christmas Day is eerily quiet, with minimal traffic and closed garages and coffee shops. The bridges in Halifax don't even collect the crossing toll on Christmas Day, and the parking garage at the hospital was free for patients' families. It's funny in times of duress how you remember the little things.

I had been concerned leaving my Dad alone in the hotel room for Christmas Eve. For good measure, I left a motion-activated singing moose in the room in my absence, as a surprise, to keep him company, and to add some much needed levity. Surprise it did, and we had a good laugh about it afterwards. He couldn't wait to share it with the grandkids.

We arrived in Halifax and went straight to the hospital to meet Mom and Dad. Mom's room was decorated with Christmas decorations given to her by the other cardiac family, and she had a super-soft, festively-themed, plush throw draped across her. I said it was for her to consider it a hug from her loved ones when we were not there. For her gift, Dad and I had specially chosen a Swarovski Crystal heart-shaped pendant necklace—a sentimental reminder of her Christmas spent in the cardiac unit—a heart for the heart patient.

We had Christmas Dinner in the hospital cafeteria—traditional turkey with all the fixings, and surprisingly tasty. Poor Mom did not fare so well—she ended up with fish for her dinner on Christmas Day. It was almost fitting for her to have such an untraditional Christmas dinner for her most untraditional Christmas.

When visiting hours were over, we made our way back to the hotel. I knew we had been upgraded to a suite for the evening but had no idea what to expect with my Christmas elves/helpers coordinating the room. It was beautiful. Heartwarmingly beautiful.

We all settled into our living-room space after changing into our comfy clothes. The adults had our cups of Christmas cheer and the kids their juice drinks, as we toasted a happy and healthy Christmas. We had our Santa hats on, and our Christmas mugs.

The tree was set up in the corner and I marveled at the festive touches around the room. It was gratifying to see the kids enjoying themselves with what was essentially a second Christmas gift opening. There was excitement and laughter—a joy in the air that was tangible, and deeply felt.

I sat in my chair, mug in hand, watching this happiness unfold around me. I had so much gratitude in my heart. We had health, we had love, and we had each other. We had the privilege of love and support from friends, family, and strangers, who pulled together to help us. I can close my eyes and still remember that utter feeling of solace.

While we didn't make it to Christmas Eve church service together, we felt the spirit of Christmas as if we were actually sitting in those church pews.

To this day, you can still see the motion activated singing Christmas moose at my parents' house along with the Christmas decorations given to us to decorate Mom's hospital room.

It was the best of times, it was the worst of times . . . . It was a special Christmas that showed humanity at its best and the real spirit of Christmas giving and kindness.

Stilly Night

Gregory Clark

This is the story of Christmas Eve 1939 for the West Novas who were crossing the North Atlantic to join the Allies in the Second World War, as told by the war correspondent who made the voyage with them. Cape Breton Highlanders were merged with the West Novas aboard the *Chrobry*.

Seven of my seventy Christmases have been spent strangely and afar. From them, I am able to prove that Christmas catches you, wherever you are. And the strangest of them was spent in the mid-winter mid-Atlantic.

Ahead of us, a half-submerged monster, the grey sea breaking over its sea-grey, surging deadliness, ploughed the British battleship *Revenge*.

To the south of us, ghostly in its lighter blue-grey, the French battleship *Dunkerque* vanished and appeared in the broken rhythm of the ocean.

Astern, the French battle cruiser *LaGloire* seemed to be keeping us in her sights.

And far and wide around us, like porpoises, the eye catching them mostly when they burst the sea on their knife edges, were the little destroyers, plunging, gliding, and seething.

What a setting for Christmas!

What a setting for five p.m. of a Christmas Eve! Watching the duck coming down, we huddled in sheltered angles of the deck of the Polish liner *Chrobry*, and no doubt thought of home.

Most of the 1,208 of us in khaki would not see home again for five years. Many of us would never see it again.

Of the 340 of us in the nondescript working clothes of the Polish merchant marine, the ship's company, all would be in the sea in less than four months, off Narvik, Norway, and the great white ship, her whiteness snarled and smeared in the grotesqueness of camouflage, would be on the bottom.

And that stately, spectral *Dunkerque*, fading to the south, what new and fateful meaning her name would have for us in less than five months! But she herself, in humbles, hiding in a little slimy North African port.

We were the second convoy of the First Canadian Division, and it was Christmas Eve, 1939.

The darkness deepened. One by one, the farther vessels vanished, no light showing anywhere.

One by one, the six other troop-laden liners melted into the night around us.

West Novas man a Lewis machine gun onboard the *Chrobry* as they cross the North Atlantic in late December 1939.

"Well?" said Andy O'Brian, the sports writer turned war correspondent for the duration.

"Let's go below," said Sammy Robertson of the Canadian Press, who three years later was to be lost at sea in another ship, torpedoed.

"Right!" said Abbie Coo, of the *Winnipeg Free Press*. "Good evening, Sir!" said I.

For around the cabin corner came Captain Deschaikowski, master of the *Chrobry*, a tall, fair, blue-eyed man like an English squire in the *Tatler*. He was unbuttoning his storm coat.

"Gentlemen," he said, "I shall see you at dinner!"

We let him go on and lingered. We were the four war correspondents with the second convoy, a little inclined to be by ourselves.

"I wonder," said Abbie Coo, "what's cooking?"

"Christmas dinner," remarked O'Brien, "on Christmas Eve?"

"It's the Polish custom," I reminded.

"To me," Sammy Robertson, in the darkness, "it's rather wonderful. These Poles, this ship's company, inviting us all for Christmas dinner! They haven't had a word from their homes, their wives, children, for four months. Since September, they have been wandering the sea like pilgrims, like the *Flying Dutchman*, homeless wherever they go. And by golly, they invite us to be their guests for Christmas dinner! The troops are to be the guests of the crew. And the officers the guests of the ship's officers . . . ."

"I wonder," I said, "what it will be like."

We went below to our cabin to freshen up. We would respond, in our best bib and tucker, to this Christmas hospitality in so improbable a situation.

The corridors of the dim-lit ship were bust with the West Novas. The unit the *Chrobry* was carrying was the West Nova Scotia Battalion, a rugged Maritime brotherhood of fishermen, miners, farmers, apple growers, not to mention drugstore clerks, store keepers, truck drivers, school teachers, schoolboys. They were thronging the corridors, heading for below decks on the big main dining saloon of the liner, all its mirrors stowed and all its pretty fixtures left in some strange port. A troop transport!

Andy O'Brien and I shared a cabin. Our door burst open.

"Holy doodle!" cried Sammy Robertson, "come on below! You should see this place!"

Down the corridors, down the stairways, we followed Sammy among the crowd of soldiers. Ahead we could hear the din of men in meeting. When we craned our way into the great saloon, there it was. Christmas.

The Poles had gone ashore, in Halifax, and laid in an enormous stack of fir and spruce, three times life-size Christmas trees that line the walls of the war-bared dining saloon of the ship, hiding its iron bones. The trees were decorated with lights, tinsel, bright coloured objects of every conceivable shape that would shine: tin, brass, clipped metal from the ship's stores. The long tables of a troop transport, unlovelier than a political picnic's, were bright with white cloths, starred with a cluster of candles.

Flowers, yes, Sir, flowers in vases.

As the West Novas, incredulous and noisy, sought their places at the tables, the Polish waiters and stewards, the crewmen not on duty above decks, the men from the purser's office and the sick bay, came from the kitchens with the Christmas feast.

It was a Polish feast. The dishes were the traditional things the lonely men would have had, if they were home. There was music and singing from them, retaliatory music and singing from the West Novas, pounding their tables. There came huge gingerbread girls, iced in colours, and the West Novas were introduced to the Polish custom of breaking these cookies among one's friends: you take a bite of mine; I'll take a bite of yours.

We four war correspondents, watching to see seven o'clock creeping up on us, when we were expected in the Captain's big dining room above, left the rising tumult, down there in the bowels of the ship, with very strange feelings in our heads and hearts.

"Come on, you fellows!" called one of the West Novas officers, "this way!"

Captain Deschaikowski was in his formal uniform, as were all his officers. They greeted the thirty, thirty-five of us from the West Novas and a few supernumeraries like ourselves, in an anteroom.

We moved into the dining cabin. It glowed with a Christmas nimbus like theirs, like ours, the evergreens, the candles, the bright colours of flowers and silver. The best china, the shining crystal, the fine wines, the feast of food, strange, Polish, gourmet. We had the traditional cookies, which we broke with our hosts. We made speeches. We sang a couple of songs.

The Revenge, Dunkerque, LaGloire, the Destroyers, the six sister transports. Outside that very door, that shrouded, curtained door, where no chink of this lovely light dare peep . . . .

So far, so good. It's a trifle before eleven o'clock. Christmas is an hour away.

Up rises the Lieutenant-Colonel commanding the West Nova Scotia Battalion, from his place on Captain Deschaikowski's right, Lt. Col. Rev. G.W. Bullock.

Reverend, did I say? Yes, Sir, yes, Madam, Reverend! Rector of the Anglican Parish of Bridgewater, Nova Scotia, who raised and recruited this battalion, and who now commands it.

"Gentlemen," says he, "may I invite you now below to the men of my battalion and the usual Christmas Eve service in the celebration of the Nativity of our Lord. Following this, the chaplain of my regiment, Captain Rev. T.F. Cashen, will conduct the Roman Catholic midnight Christmas Mass."

This is the truth. The truth of Christmas Eve aboard the Polish ship *Chrobry* in the year 1939.

We went below. And in the big dining saloon where the troops had finished their dinner, the altar had been set up.

And the Lieutenant-Colonel commanding the West Nova Scotia Battalion put on his surplice and vestments over his soldier's uniform and conducted the office of the Anglican prayer book that marks the Nativity of our Lord. And no man in the jammed ship's great belly moved.

And when the Lieutenant-Colonel commanding removed his vestments and surplice and took his place among his men, the battalion's chaplain, the priest, Father Cashen, stepped up to the same altar, laid out on it his linen and his missal and his little golden chalice, and while no man moved of us all, began the midnight Christmas Mass.

And that, my friends in the midnight Atlantic, and that winter gale, and those unseen ships plunging with us on a long, far errand, was my ecumenical Christmas.

Rev. Bullock, due to his age, was unable to command the West Nova Scotia Regiment in the field. He reverted to the rank of Captain in order to follow them to Italy in 1943, in a graves registration unit. He had the sad duty of burying his own son, Reg. Mortally wounded on

Christmas Day, near Ortona in 1943, Reg had commanded the mortar platoon of the West Nova Scotia Regiment.

Into a New Country

Mike Finigan

December 27. And already the Christmas tree seems different. It's like an old, valued colleague who retired six months ago but keeps coming by to say hi and see how that McComber file is going.

Still, one can sit, watch the lights for an evening: reflect. Take a blow.

Let's see.

On Christmas Eve we went to church in Sydney River, the place was packed, and we watched the brilliant children's Nativity story.

At home somebody got a hand puppet chicken for Christmas and now I'm learning how to talk without moving my lips.

I didn't have a Christmas gift-wrap bonfire this year. I learned my lesson last year after spending the first two weeks of the New Year blind in bed with acute lung infection.

Bad idea. Pretty flames, though.

Wiggle the toes. Pat the cat. Finish off the season with a turkey sandwich and cranberry sauce. Mittful of cashews. More chocolates.

Nothing to do but sit here and gaze. Unbuzz.

Which requires considerable patience.

It's hard to be still and stop twitching and blinking for ten minutes in these jittery times. But I got a book on meditation for Christmas that should help.

"Close your eyes and see the tree."

Yes. I understand.

We got our tree on December first. A lot of people balk at that idea. They argue the aesthetic decline of a month-old fir. But it's never been a problem.

A tree that hangs around long enough, like an old friend, looks the same over time anyway. Pounds and needles go unnoticed.

Though I am aware that by January first it's possible I'll flick a switch and the tree will explode into flames.

The thing is, the problem would be not getting a tree on December first. Tree talk starts here on November twelfth and it builds and gathers momentum like rumours of a snow day.

The anticipation is dizzying. People get cranky and short in a treeless Advent.

We do get a real tree. You might prefer an artificial tree. A plastic puppy with searchlights, that plays Elvis tunes and says, "Thank you. Thank you very much," when you walk by. Doesn't matter, you're still using the opportunity to bring a whole tree—well, minus the roots—indoors, put lights on it, stick it in the corner and watch it.

For fun.

Everything doesn't have to make sense in life. Everything doesn't have to add up. Sometimes one must give fun its due. It does have its merits.

I went through a period of cynicism there that lasted a good fifteen years, a waste, but eventually I returned to the notion of eking a little fun out of life.

Still, I don't think I'll be snapping on my Speedo and jumping off the South Bar wharf on New Year's Day, fun though it might be. I prefer to take my mirth in less chancy temperatures.

I'm just saying. To be born is to be thrown into the now frigid, now cordial, waters of life up to your eyeballs.

Sometimes we're in way over our head; sometimes we're just staying afloat. Other times we get on swimmingly.

My favourite prophet Ecclesiastes said: "There's a time to mourn and a time to dance." That's the deal. Me? I'd like to have the courage and wisdom to accept those terms with equanimity. Go about living large, unafraid.

The urging of all prophets, "Be not afraid."

A tall order.

In the coming New Year I say give the dance its due.

My hero, Gus McCrae, a fictional imaginary hero I guess, of Larry McMurtry's novel *Lonesome Dove*, once said:

"I can't think of nothing better than riding a fine horse into a new Country."

Here's to new starts and future Christmas trees.

Be bold. Be kind. Saddle up.

Christmas with a Muslim

Sharon Dunn

Christmas was coming and I mentioned to my Iranian boyfriend that I had to start getting ready. He knew that Christmas involved a tree, but I figured that was pretty much all that he knew. He was very Muslim. I had even asked him if it was okay in his religion to date me. "Not only that," he said, "Muslims are allowed to marry Christians and Jews." Good to know, I replied, and we laughed.

I got busy with other things and Christmas went on the back burner, until one day when he showed up at my door lugging a huge and real Christmas tree. "Good lord," I said, "I haven't had a real tree since I was a kid and I've never had one that big." I was less than thrilled. "I wanted to get you the best possible tree," he said, "do you like it?" "I love it," I lied, wondering where it would fit and how many bulbs I was going to have to buy to decorate the monstrosity.

He left it in the middle of the floor and was gone. I rolled my eyes and groaned, just what I needed two days before Christmas.

An hour later, he was back lugging another large tree, this one a silver ornamental "fake" tree. "What are you doing?' I asked him, aghast. "You said you were accustomed to artificial trees, so I wanted to get you one of those too," he smiled, "after all, this is a big occasion."

Now I had two large trees to decorate and I wasn't happy about it. He spent the rest of the day getting the real tree set up. "It really needs water," he said. Well, at least he wasn't leaving it flat out, dying on the floor for me to take care of. "I'll put the silver one up tomorrow," he promised.

I ran around the next day. It was Christmas Eve and I was doing last minute shopping, as usual. When I got home, he had the artificial tree up as well. And he had already put the lights on both trees—clear white for the silver and multicolor for the real tree. Thank god he had taken care of the hard stuff.

I noticed a number of small velvet boxes.

"What are these?" I asked. "I bought them for you," he replied. I opened the first one. It was the most intricate, beautiful tree decoration I had ever seen—Mary and her baby in the manger. It was exquisite. The remainder of the boxes contained similar items—all beautiful and expensive—and all religious themed.

"I don't get it," I told him. "None of this means anything to you. Why didn't you just buy cheap bulbs, like I usually do?"

"Sharon Dunn," he admonished me. "My religion sees Jesus as a prophet from God. This is a very important night."

He insisted that on such a special occasion, of course he

would get the best and most meaningful bulbs. "This is my first Christmas and it's with you. I want to get it right," he said.

I was happy when he started decorating the tree—not a job I like. He did all of the decorating himself; it took him hours. He took such great care that in the end, I had two of the most beautiful Christmas trees on the planet, compliments of a Muslim.

That evening I put the presents under the tree. My sons were grown and out of the country, arriving on Christmas Day—so this Christmas Eve, it was him and me. He came to the door dressed up for the evening. I had never seen him dressed up before. "I am honoured that you are allowing me to be part of this night," he said. He was carrying a sack with something huge in it, wrapped in paper bags. It was my gift. I put it under the tree. I had a slew of gifts for him, so I had him open them first—starting with a beautiful cashmere sweater.

"I can't accept this, Sharon Dunn," he said upon inspection. "It costs too much money. I will never accept anything of monetary value from you." I tried but I couldn't talk him into it.

"Well, you're going to love your stocking then," I assured him, "since I'm the queen of cheap Christmas stockings."

He opened his stocking gifts with ohh's and aah's over chocolate, an orange, an apple, deodorant, socks, and a slinky.

"I love everything," he enthused, "especially the deodorant." It wasn't a hint, I assured him. "I forgot to buy it today, this is so great," he insisted.

"Stop being excited about the deodorant," I complained, as he dug in for the last gift in the toe. He was going to love this one. It was from Tiffany's. He had bought me a beautiful ring from there once, and I knew that he had loved this ring for men at the time we were there.

He eyed it carefully.

"It's beautiful, Sharon Dunn," he said. "Is it real or is it a fake?" "It's real of course," I told him. "Then you have to take it back," he said, putting it down and adding, "You can get me a knock off on Amazon for five dollars next Christmas, and I will cherish it. But," he added, "the deodorant, now that was the perfect gift."

Now it was my turn. He handed me his awkwardly wrapped gift. It was heavy. I opened the layers of paper and—voila!—"A very large sword?" "It's very old," he told me. "It does look old," I agreed. "Do you like it?," he asked hopefully. "Well, I'll tell you," I replied, "I can honestly say that I've never had anything like this before, and it might really come in handy one day."

He was pleased with my reaction.

I asked him what the sword symbolized in his ancient and colourful heritage. "In my faith, a sword means strength in battle, but Sharon, in your Christian faith, it symbolizes the power and goodness of your god and that's what we're celebrating tonight! Your god, but also my prophet."

We had a wonderful evening. It was so magical and it was all because of him. I was blown away by the respect and dignity he had given to a holiday that even I, raised a Catholic, had seen turned commercial so many years earlier. It struck me that it's not enough to just tolerate and maybe even enjoy another person's culture and beliefs, like I always did, but to go the extra mile, like he did—to learn about it. To actually show such respect was astounding to me.

I still cherish that special evening and the lessons a Muslim taught me about the real meaning of my own Christian Christmas.

The *Cape Breton's Christmas*
books, 1 through 10,
are all available
in stores and at
www.capebretonbooks.com
or phone 1-800-565-5140

Breton Books
Wreck Cove, Cape Breton, Nova Scotia B0C 1H0
bretonbooks@gmail.com • 1-800-565-5140
www.capebretonbooks.com